6.50

9

14

3

22

The Accidental Explorer

ALSO BY SHERRY SIMPSON

The Way Winter Comes: Alaska Stories

THE ACCIDENTAL EXPLORER

Wayfinding in Alaska

SHERRY SIMPSON

SASQUATCH BOOKS
SEATTLE

Several of these essays originally appeared in slightly different form in *The Anchorage Press*, including "A Man Made Cold by the Universe," "Turning Back," "The Mapmaker," "Impedimenta," and "The Undiscovered Place." "A Man Made Cold by the Universe" was also published in the online journal *Nidus: A Journal of Contemporary Art and Literature* (Spring 2003), in *The Alaska Reader: Voices from the North* (Fulcrum Publishing, 2005), and in *Travelers' Tales Alaska: True Stories* as "I Want to Ride in the Bus Chris Died In" (Travelers' Tales, 2003). "Turning Back" was published in *Going Alone: Women's Adventures in the Wild* (Seal Press, 2004). "Fidelity" appeared in the Winter 2004 issue of *Pilgrimage*.

Printed in the United States of America
Published by Sasquatch Books
Distributed by PGW/Perseus
15 14 13 12 11 10 09 08   9 8 7 6 5 4 3 2 1

Cover photograph: © James Kay
Cover design: Rosebud Eustace
Interior design: Jessica Norton
Interior composition: Sarah Plein

Library of Congress Cataloging-in-Publication Data

Simpson, Sherry.
 The accidental explorer : wayfinding in Alaska / Sherry Simpson.
  p. cm.
 ISBN-13: 978-1-57061-537-5
 ISBN-10: 1-57061-537-3
 1. Alaska--Description and travel--Anecdotes. 2. Alaska--History--Anecdotes. 3. Adventure and adventurers--Alaska--Anecdotes. 4. Outdoor life--Alaska--Anecdotes. 5. Wilderness areas--Alaska--Anecdotes. 6. Simpson, Sherry--Travel--Alaska. I. Title.

F904.6.S56 2008
917.9804'52--dc22

                    2007044490

Sasquatch Books
119 South Main Street, Suite 400
Seattle, WA 98104
(206) 467-4300
www.sasquatchbooks.com
custserv@sasquatchbooks.com

For the first adventurers I ever knew:
Mom, Dad, and Aunt Chris.

Contents

And life has thus been searched and exploited almost everywhere all lands over, except: Among us who seek on enchanted rivers an answer to those underthoughts that make life at once a tragic and ecstatic thing, who dare for nothing but the cause of daring, who follow the long trails.

—ROBERT DUNN, *The Shameless Diary of an Explorer*

Introduction

YEARS AGO A SECRET BOOK EXISTED behind the counter of the hotel in Denali National Park. A friend who worked there showed it to me once. The tattered cover read: "Official Black Book. Enter all silly questions and other strange things within." For season after season, bemused hotel clerks had recorded unusual inquiries made by park visitors. The book was a compendium of disappointment and confusion, inked in scribbles of various colors and urgency:

"What time do you turn on the Northern Lights?"

"Where do they keep the animals in winter?"

"Do bears lay eggs?"

"What do we do on the second day here?"

"When do they let the animals out?"

"Is the park open to everybody or just to tourists?"

I memorized some of the questions so I could repeat them at parties. It was easy to mock tourists who visited Alaska for a few days and then left, probably forever, never quite certain of what they'd seen and why they'd come. If these questions represented their abiding mysteries, I couldn't imagine what on earth they'd discover here.

"How come the mountain is so far away from the park?"

"Where's my wife?"

"How much does Mount McKinley weigh without the snow?"

"How many undiscovered lakes are there in the park?"

"But if you don't have radio, TV, telephones, tennis courts, or a swimming pool, what is there to do?"

One question haunts me still. The "Official Black Book" describes an old man who approached the desk to ask, "How far do I have to go before I can say I've been there?"

I wish I had been the scribe who, upon hearing his riddle, copied the words in careful script onto the book's lined pages before stepping around the counter to take the pilgrim's arm. "Yes, my friend," I'd murmur, leading him gently away. "Wouldn't we all like to know?"

And together we would push through the hotel's double doors and into the unknown world, as if we could discover the answer and return to tell everyone else.

I was born in Santa Fe, New Mexico, as were my father and my sister. Our family moved eleven times before I turned seven. I attended three first grades: in Utah, in Colorado, in Virginia.

I remember the July day we arrived in Juneau, Alaska, the way the barnacle must regard its final and lasting attachment, with relief and a niggling worry: Is *this* the place?

The following summer we lived in Mount McKinley National Park, as it then was known. My father, a civil engineer, was in charge of a project to pave the first fifteen miles of the park road as far as the Savage River. For three months, we lived at park headquarters, a modest compound of log buildings built in 1925 and newer government housing. We wedged ourselves into a trailer so small that the four kids shared two bunks embedded in the hallways like Pullman sleepers. I slept with my sister's feet in my face the entire summer.

How I envied the few children who lived in the park year-round. They schooled at home with their mothers and mailed lessons to a correspondence teacher in Juneau. My friend Julie showed me the picture she'd drawn of a lynx that appeared near their house one winter, which her teacher endorsed with an enthusiastic A. Probably it seemed to me that Julie had been graded not on her artistic abilities but on being lucky enough to live in a place where lynxes snowshoed about on furred paws and speared innocent creatures with an amber glance.

Julie's older brother knocked together a tiny log cabin on the slope above Rock Creek just beyond the houses. We chinked the gaps between peeling spruce timbers with fragrant moss and tacked flowered fabric across the crudely notched window. I imagined living there through winter, when snow fell so deep it buried the world. Like the romantic I would forever be, the practicalities of making heat and gathering food never occurred to me. In the spring I would burrow out like a bear, blinking in the light.

That summer the sun never set long enough for true darkness to fall, and no matter how tightly we pressed curtains against the porthole in the bunk bed, brightness buckled around the edges as I lay trapped in false twilight, restlessly shoving against my sister's legs. Surely my parents had rules, but in a place without playgrounds or fences or ball fields, it's no wonder my strongest memories feature me as an orphaned, half-feral child roaming freely from adventure to adventure, discoveries all around.

This, then, was the child becoming herself. I pounded dull cubes of fool's gold free from granite rocks. Dug green bones of snowshoe hares from beneath a duff of dry spruce needles. Chucked arrows at makeshift targets. Felt the blast of my heart when I woke from daydreaming to see an impassive moose standing before me. Heard the drum of my feet against the damp trail as I ran away. Tasted the sour burst of blueberries picked warm and dusty. Scuffed through the silvered ruins of some long-dead prospector's cabin.

This is how I discovered my home. This was my first act of wayfinding.

Sometimes, though, we lose our way, without ever realizing it. The summer in Mount McKinley ended, and my mother drove the station wagon along washboard gravel roads through mountain passes and tundra plains to a ferry that scooped us in and floated us back to Juneau. We lived in the Mendenhall Valley, hedged by a glacier at one end and tidal flats at the other. Year by year, more and more people like us fell like cabbages off a conveyor belt that rolled ceaselessly from the province we called "Outside." On this suburban frontier I grew up climbing trees in a rain forest and riding motorcycles on back roads scraped from glacial till. I camped with friends on uninhabited beaches and stood in line for *Star Wars*, fished with my dad off Shelter Island and played third-string basketball in high school, ate (reluctantly) ocean-bright salmon two or three times a week and Kraft macaroni and cheese when we were lucky.

I never became the sort of Alaskan who flies planes, kills wild animals, fishes open seas, climbs mountains, or treks through the backcountry as if it were no more troublesome than driving to the local 7-Eleven for a newspaper. Nobody I knew then made long, aimless excursions into the backcountry. That would require arranging vacation time, paying dearly for plane charters, and suffering unusual privations and unforeseen difficulties. Such pursuits might have signaled a lack of something more useful to do with your time.

Besides, life seemed interesting enough in a place where the separation between nature and home seemed no more substantial than the faint rattle of a beaded curtain between doorways. Black bears strolled through backyards. Humpback whales coursed silently like intergalactic freighters beneath my father's boat. The Mendenhall Glacier was a grand blue slab of scenery for thousands of thrilled tourists and a playground where everyday hooligans like me spent afternoons leaping off moraines and plinking rocks at castaway icebergs.

There were moments that scraped away this unmindfulness. After a night of babysitting, for instance, I sat on the house's cold concrete steps to watch the 4 a.m. dawn pinking the clouds behind Thunder Mountain, and some foreknowledge of a larger world both frightening and exhilarating pierced me. On a day in November, huddled in dead grasses on the Mendenhall wetlands, I watched Canada geese so intently through binoculars that the tide rose unnoticed and stranded me, and it was not so much the bitter cold but some recognition of life's blind passage that made me cry as I waded through chest-deep water toward solid ground. Another morning, at Eagle River, as I stood within a copse of trees, a carillon of hidden ravens showered me with glottal chimes and watery knocks, and something in their dark enchantment made me grateful and afraid.

Of course I could never have used the words *home* or *wilderness* then with any awareness of their complicated meanings, nor did I know the phrase *mysterium tremendum*, a German theologian's term for *awe-fullness*, *numinous dread*, an apprehension of the *Other*. Years fell behind me, miles passed beneath my feet, before I recognized that such moments—and how painfully few they are—help us recognize *axis mundi*, the center of the world, which is not a place but a way of being. Like wilderness. Like home.

And so I came late to adventure, or perhaps adventure came late to me. At twelve, I would lie on my belly in the living room with forearms anchoring a slick map of North America, tracing a water route from the Mississippi River to the Pacific, tributary by stream by creek. It was Sacagawea who interested me. She'd known the way, and what she knew could not be separated from who she was and how she lived. But not until my thirties did I make a backcountry trip that involved anything more challenging than a night shivering in a soggy tent with girlfriends, unhinged by terrified giggles at the prowling of imaginary bears around us. Living in Alaska is not about tempting trouble but about avoiding it whenever possible. The goal of wilderness travel is "to *not* have adventures," I once heard a field scientist say.

For me, adventure sprang first, as most discovery does, from an act of imagination, born from an ignorance no less laughable than that of any tourist wondering who switches on the aurora, or what secret zoo houses wild animals until summer. I took a job in graduate school mapping historic trails for a governor and his retainers who did not believe in wilderness, because to them the word translated as a "lockup" of land and resources by the federal government. The governor's people regarded wilderness as a bank vault crammed with oil, coal, natural gas, gold, silver, zinc, timber, and a few lesser currencies, like scenery. "We can't just let nature run wild," the governor said to remind us that resource extraction was a divine right. All the state needed to retrieve these treasures were the legal rights-of-way attached to more than a thousand old trails webbing the landscape. "We're Alas-*cans*, not Alas-*can'ts!*" the lieutenant governor said to encourage our efforts.

My conscience troubled me on this job until we researchers realized that this project and the creaky federal statute it exploited were headed nowhere except the courts, which would grind away at the legalities until the sun collapsed into charcoal. Nobody really knew which trails still persisted out there, anyway, in a landscape that never ceased changing.

Before long, I didn't believe in the existence of wilderness either—not, anyway, the kind that the Wilderness Act described as "untrammeled by man." Examining old maps and plundering historic records convinced me there was no creek in

Alaska that had not been frisked by miners, no valley unhunted by Natives or whites, no expanse uncrossed by foot or dog team or tractor. I know of only one contemporary map of Alaska unmarked by lines incising official wildernesses, refuges, parks, ownerships, roads, trails, cities, villages. It is stripped of names, radiantly deceitful in all its green and glorious falsehoods, its pretense of innocence, its celebration of an unpeopled landscape, its portrayal of an Alaska that has never existed.

When our supervisor commanded us to document proof of a trail's existence at the average rate of one per day, the other researchers and I formed a factory line to package history as neatly as a butcher wraps meat in plastic trays. We replicated hundreds of antique trails onto inch-to-the-mile topographic maps. That's how I spent a few summers and winters, laboring beneath the chilly cast of fluorescent lights, blithely skipping my pencil over ridges and through muskeg, guessing at passes, ascending slopes, avoiding bluffs, crossing rivers and rounding lakes, rejoicing whenever I encountered a dashed line no more substantial than an ant's footprints, because it suggested the thinnest possibility that *out there*, in the almost wilderness, under a different sky, someone had gone just far enough to prove his own existence.

"You could go there, too," he might as well have whispered as I folded maps into origami and organized fat files to await court or oblivion, whichever came first. Or perhaps it was I who did the whispering.

For an obsessive and expensive period, I bought my own rare maps, trying to assemble an atlas of dreams past. Earlier than the hopeful gold rush maps, before the geological survey maps, there is a modest 1797 map of North America that shows a confident Atlantic coastline cleaving onto the uncertain outlines of the Pacific. Alaska hovers in the distance, fetal in its soft misshapenness, the border halting at Icy Cape as if the mapmaker actually had plunged into the fabled abyss at the world's edge. Nobody knew where Alaska began or ended. It strikes me today as the most accurate map we have.

For my birthday one year I begged my husband to buy me an edition of the *Compilation of Narratives of Explorations in Alaska*, published by the government in 1900, so I wouldn't be tempted to steal one from the library, which seemed to have an extra copy or two. Unlike the false geographers who divined the shapes of continents entirely from imagination, the early nineteenth-century explorers sent north by the U.S. Army charted only what they experienced. These mapmakers scrupulously recorded their ignorance on page after page by showing what they didn't know, a testament to the weakness of feet but strength of heart, the limits of vision, the uneasiness of these journeys. On these silken panels, disembodied peaks and foothills resemble magnetized iron filings. Elsewhere, notations startle: the word "flat" or sometimes "flat and low," an eagle's nest fixed on this river bend, graves along that slough, an Athabascan Indian camp perched above a bank. Every time I studied these vast tracts of creamy paper, I couldn't help but suspect the land itself was blank until the cartographers conjured it into existence by laying eyes upon it and making it real. The charts seduced me into believing I'd be extending their discoveries, encountering wilderness, if I retraced those narrow journeys myself.

This, of course, was a fancy for which I'd been primed all my life, through stories and histories and movies relating again and again the heroic adventures of explorers ever pushing westward and northerly. The discoverer's task was to inventory the land, subdue it, possess it. What once was empty, on the map and in the mind, would be rendered safe and knowable simply by inscribing it with familiar names, trails, trade routes, settlements—all the useful templates that had served so well before.

In Alaska, the Original Peoples became another inventory item, rarely hostile and often generous, saving numerous adventurers from starvation, poor judgment, or ignorance. In return, the explorers and those who followed never truly saw their presence on the land, *with* the land. You have only to read manifestos by those trying to protect the Arctic National Wildlife Refuge to see how strongly this resistance operates even now. "[T]he area conservationists call 'wilderness' is often as remote and foreign to local Natives as say a lawn is to a suburban home owner . . ." writes Paul Ongtooguk, an educator and scholar who is Inupiat.

Anyone can identify a lawn, but to locate "wilderness" is trickier. I consulted the writings of brave scholars who seemed as engaging and contrary as ravens squabbling over french fries. Thus, I learned that wilderness is a cultural construct; a place seemingly untouched by humans; a reservoir of spiritual renewal; a metaphor for dark and godless chaos; an uninhabited wasteland; an elitist playground; an idea existing beyond society and history; an illusion; a myth; an invention; a necessity; a pretense; a blank spot on the map that we must either fill or forever leave empty; a stage upon which we play out melodramas of identity, ownership, and dominance; a touchstone; a refuge; a resource; a luxury; our first experience; our last hope.

We say that wilderness is preserved, conserved, bordered, set aside, withdrawn, elevated, administered, protected, expanded, managed, untouched, diminished, undeveloped, valued, devalued, revered, reviled, exploited, privileged, experienced, polluted, diluted, pristine, marketed, sustained, legislated, and designated.

To use quotation marks around these definitions would only amplify the ironic distance between idea and actuality, between the rubbery taste of empty words in your mouth and the way it feels to stand alone beneath some big sky, part of an unsparing landscape that unaccountably enlarges you, knowing that miles and days separate you from some other life you used to lead, some other person you used to be. To me the term "wilderness" became so fraught with multiple intentions and cultural significance that handling it reminded me of basic gun safety: be careful where you point it and always assume it's loaded. The more I read, the more certain it seemed I would never accidentally encounter wilderness, much less deliberately. I might not even recognize it if I ever saw it.

This is not to say I gave up trying. I once wrote down a notion that surfaced while I stood on a modest mountaintop on Admiralty Island. "I thought I might be the first person to set foot there," I wrote. (The presumption makes me cringe today.) A friend noted in the margin, "Why do people always want to be the *first person* to stand in a place?" And why would they assume they were the first person at all, she might have added.

What a relief, then, to learn that Alaska's Original Peoples have no comparable concept of wilderness because the word suggests a landscape untouched by humans, and such an untruth implies a lack of reciprocity between the natural, human, and spiritual worlds. The detachment between land and self is unfathomable. What Euro-Americans see as wilderness, Natives see as homeland. This was the only discovery I'd made in years.

Since I was a child, I've wished I'd been born in Alaska, so that my connection would seem implicit, and not something I'm always trying to force, like the caulk that seals the ship's planks, the knot that clasps the rope to itself. The older I get, the harder it becomes to see the wilderness I want to return to, the home I need to belong to. How, then, to reconcile these notions—not between explorers and the Original Peoples— but within myself?

It was Robert Dunn, author of *The Shameless Diary of an Explorer*, who saved me from despair. He chronicled the first failed effort of Frederick Cook to summit Denali in 1903, undercutting every pretense at noble aspiration simply by telling truths about his companions and himself. And yet, he understood the reason why anyone sets off across an unknown landscape. "The true spirit of an explorer is a primordial restlessness," he wrote. He added, "It is a creative instinct."

Surely an explorer would have recognized the passionate ignorance of my earliest and mostly pointless ambitions. I studied maps, read accounts, made notes, tried to talk friends into joining me. Why *not* traverse the Alaska-Canada border, top to bottom, or maybe bottom to top? Wasn't it time somebody retraced the epic fifteen-hundred-mile trek of Lt. Henry Allen into Alaska's center (though how to accomplish that bit in which his expedition traveled up the Copper River in a boat made from moose skin was a bit of a problem)? Perhaps it would be easier to walk the entire coast of Alaska, outlining its rim step by step.

But this alone convinced me to set out on my adventures: unless I moved beyond the world as I thought I knew it, unless I set myself on some journey, however small, how could I ever reconcile this constant restlessness with the desire to know and love one place? How would I ever recognize home unless I could find my way there through a wilderness? I didn't have to define it. I'd know it when I found it.

So off I went, into Glacier Bay to seek naturalist John Muir's source of divinity, through the Kantishna country to stand at the foot of Denali, and along a gold rush trail in interior Alaska. I hiked a remote Pacific coast inhabited only by bears and journeyed to the abandoned bus where Christopher McCandless found slow death and sudden fame. I rummaged through the lives of other wanderers, studying the letters of a former explorer who rooted himself in the Yukon Flats. And along the way, there were other adventures, other places, other stories. Those chronicled here are just a few.

In the old Alaska accounts, explorers often mention the accuracy of Native representations of the landscape, yet few of these maps exist. It was years before I understood they were not meant to. Contemporary geographer Robert Rundstrom writes that the Inuit were mappers, not mapmakers, recounting how an elder explained that he had drawn intricate maps from memory but had thrown them away long before. "It was the act of making them that was important, the recapitulation of environmental features, not the material objects themselves," Rundstrom explained.

On my maps, I carefully marked campsites and daily mileages and false routes. Not one map plots what it was like to fall into a glacial river, face a threatening bear, or agonize over when to abandon a solo hike. None shows how to navigate the perils of daily life: the losses of a house fire, the contemplation of death, the healing of an endangered marriage. No map ever recorded a place named HOME.

The act, the recapitulation, the knowingness. The mapping, not the map. The finding, not the found.

This is how I think of us, we adventurers, explorers, and tourists. We are all standing on the tundra looking into the blue distance. We wear windbreakers and sneakers, and some of us even have name tags so we won't get lost and forget who we are. Others peer through cameras and camcorders, trying to find something familiar to photograph to show the folks back home. A few rummage through backpacks, hoping they brought the proper gear for their ascents, descents, journeys, passages, and pilgrimages. Here and there people bend over to study the complicated life swelling greenly around their feet. Just a few begin to walk across the yielding ground, toward whatever surprising thing lies just beyond our vision. And there I am, falling to my knees on the tundra, hoping once again that this is the place.

A Nuisance to Myself and Others

It was the third night of our kayak trip in Glacier Bay, or maybe the fourth. I forget now. Jennifer and I had crawled into the damp grotto of the tent and scrunched deep into our sleeping bags. Inches from my face, the tent wall sagged from the steady rain, the inner surface slick with condensation. The blue tarp we'd tossed in desperation over the rain fly rustled ceaselessly in the wind and cast a dim glacial light inside.

"I haven't been to bed by 8:15 p.m. since second grade," Jennifer said. It wasn't dark and wouldn't be for hours, and these facts combined with the clamminess—my hair, my socks, my sleeping bag—meant plenty of time to lie there feeling chilled and miserable before sleep arrived. If sleep arrived.

I struggled to turn the pages of John Muir's *Travels in Alaska* while wearing gloves. He'd journeyed up this very inlet more than a century before, indulging a slightly dotty interest in glaciers. I noted with satisfaction his complaints of "crouching cramped and benumbed in the canoe, poulticed in wet or damp clothing night and day." *Poulticed.* That was the word. But his remedy for discomfort was a fifteen-hundred-foot hike up a mountain through more rain, mud, and shoulder-deep snow in search of a panoramic view. It was maddening how much time Muir spent bounding through stark mountains and crossing dangerous glaciers with gladness and glory swelling his heart. He began sentences with phrases such as "Dancing down the mountain to camp, my mind glowing like the sunbeaten glaciers . . ." and concluded adventures with statements such as "After my twelve-mile walk, I ate a cracker and planned the camp."

He must have been delusional, a fraud, or one hell of a kidder. I put the book down and tried to doze despite the percussive rain and the crackling tarp, the malodorous vapors of sweaty polypro, the recognition that tomorrow we'd spend another day here, and another, and another, the irritating knowledge that this was no one's idea but my own.

There is an amusing story related by the Greek historian Arrian: "On the appearance of Alexander and his army, these venerable men stamped [the earth] with their feet and gave no other sign of interest. Alexander asked through interpreters what they meant by this odd behavior, and they replied: 'King Alexander, every man can possess only so much of this earth's surface as this we are standing on. You are but human like the rest of us, save that you are always busy . . . traveling so many miles from your home, a nuisance to yourself and to others.'"

John Muir took credit for discovering Glacier Bay in 1879, though historians note that, technically speaking, several others visited or noted the bay's existence as early as 1794, and the Huna Tlingits point out that, technically speaking, what was there to discover? They had been collecting seabird eggs and eating the sweet, rich flesh and oil of harbor seals and gathering berries in the homeland they called *Sitakaday*, "the bay where the ice was," for who knows how long before that mischievous girl Kaasteen whistled the ice down from the mountains, forcing the people to flee until eventually the glaciers retreated. But that's their story, not Muir's and not mine.

So let's just say Muir was the first to describe Glacier Bay in print, the first to urge everyone else to come have a look-see. Muir had traveled up the Inside Passage by steamship, hoping to compare Alaska's glaciers with his ideas about the Sierra Nevada. Prospectors assured him the best glaciers existed along the passage's northerly channels. In Fort Wrangell, the evangelist S. Hall Young helped him locate a canoe and crew willing to travel in mid-October, which traditionally produces weather contemporary residents most often describe as "crappy."

The crew's names were given as Toyatte and John from the Stickeens, Kadachan from the Chilkats, and Sitka Charley. Young accompanied Muir to spread the word of Christianity among the Natives, a movement then advancing throughout Alaska as inexorably as a glacier. Along the way, Muir rambled through the rain forest, discussed with his companions the nature of wolves' souls, sketched totem poles, and occasionally gave diffident speeches of gratitude and admiration to clans that hosted them, joking with the Huna Tlingit, for example, to "find a better use for missionaries than putting them, like salmon, in pots for food." Such good intentions, such single-mindedness, such ignorance. Did he ever once see *Lingít Aaní*, Tlingit country? What did he know of their language, their ancestors, their understanding of the fish and birds and creatures? No more than I did.

It was Sitka Charley who mentioned seal hunting as a boy in a "bay of ice-mountains," oddly desolate of trees and dominated by colossal glaciers. Charley knew he could find this place again, and he did. Just inside the entrance, the travelers encountered Huna seal hunters gathering food for winter. Muir wanted information about the bay; the hunters wondered what these strangers could possibly want here so late in the year. Charley finally convinced a hunter to guide them for pay. This unnamed person is the one who could tell us something about the incomprehensibility of an explorer's compulsions. Muir notes that the seal hunter's wife saw them off with these words: "It is my husband that you are taking away. See that you bring him back." Thus we are reminded of the explorer's corollary: somewhere, someone waits while you traipse about on your mysterious errands.

For mile after mile of choppy waves, the paddlers thrust the canoe toward great broken wedges of ice bluing the horizon. Muir gazed at shadowy peaks rearing upward from the shore as the Tlingits bent their backs to the work, bare hands clutching the paddles. "The wind was in our favor," Muir wrote, "but a cold rain pelted us, and we could see but little of the dreary, treeless wilderness which we had now fairly entered." At every encampment, the others waited beside a gloomy fire while Muir climbed alone into the clouds, as was his habit, seeking views best appreciated in solitude, exulting in light prismed by snow and ice into radiance, swallowed by visions of cold wildness unspeakably pure and sublime. This was what he had really come to experience: the face of God.

Muir described their departure from the bay this way:

> *We turned and sailed away, joining the outgoing bergs, while "Gloria in Excelsis" still seemed to be sounding over all the white landscape, and our burning hearts were ready for any fate, feeling that whatever the future might have in store, the treasures we had gained this glorious morning would enrich our lives forever.*

Glory and destiny, just fifty miles east from my hometown. Why had I waited so long? This was my first backcountry trip, my first long kayak paddle. I had no idea what I was doing. I wasn't sure if Jennifer, a white-water kayaker and mother of three small girls, had joined me through an interest in Muir, in glaciers, or in a week's reprieve from little voices and grasping hands. All I knew was the line I'd sketched on the map, descriptions that pointed thataway, the certainty that by following Muir I would discover treasures, enrichment, a burning heart ready for any fate.

Here is some of what happened to us on our minor expedition:

After the backcountry boat dropped us off at Sebree Island at the inlet's mouth, the other kayakers tossed their boats into the water and sped away, churning the water like scoters launching themselves into flight. Jennifer and I were marooned, baffled by the blue rubbery hide and wooden skeleton of the Klepper kayak, a small whale we needed to reconstitute. I'd carefully penciled instructions as Jennifer's husband assembled and disassembled the collapsible boat so deftly on that sunny lawn back in Fairbanks; now the directions appeared to be written in Sanskrit.

The only lingering kayakers, a French couple visiting Alaska, pushed us aside, tsking over our incompetence and the fallibility of German design. There is no pity like French pity. Our image of ourselves as tough Alaskans—Jennifer was born in Fairbanks, and I'd grown up beside the ocean, for God's sake—turned out to be as collapsible as the boat, and more difficult to reconstruct.

We also had forgotten the kayak's rudder, the spray skirts that would seal us into the boat and shut the waves out, and a tide table to help us time our departures. These oversights meant we spent most of our trip zigzagging, bailing, and paddling against the current.

That first day seemed so promising—flat water that mirrored a pewter sky, a charm of seals that followed the kayak. The campsite offered just a few disadvantages. Two men tenting down the beach did not mind openly dropping their trousers on the low tide. Crazed black flies orbited our faces as we ate. A portable propane heater I'd bought to stave off hypothermia sputtered and died on first use, becoming instant ballast. But we pitched our tent in a meadow of lupine and chocolate lily, sure we'd find our rhythm once we left people behind.

The next day, the rain began. It rained every day after that. Most days the wind blew, too. This was not the soft rain of "good quality" that Muir rhapsodized about. Of course I knew it rained in Southeast Alaska—my mother had urged us to play outside whenever the sun broke through so we wouldn't develop rickets—but this was the hard, cold rain that chills the soul as well as the body. This was rain you couldn't escape, only endure.

With the rain came further trials, minor but amplifying, like swells surging into whitecaps. My dry suit sprang a leak, so that I spent much of the trip with a soggy rear end. Jennifer slashed her hand with a knife and spent much of the trip with a finger wrapped in damp, bloody gauze. Everything we brought grew wetter and wetter, and everything we wore got smellier and smellier. I peppered our food heavily to disguise the perpetual grind of sand between the teeth. One afternoon Jennifer spontaneously tested the can of bear repellent spray against the wind, and a fiery veil of red pepper laminated our faces for the rest of the day.

When I saw bear dung by our campsite, I said nothing.

Tired of sitting in the rain, oppressed by the hovering layer of clouds, we cocooned ourselves in the tent rather than huddle around a cook pot or attempt one more beleaguered fire. Convinced we heard many, many bears pacing along the beach, each turning with interest toward the tent, we warbled sketchy versions of Episcopalian hymns (Jennifer) and the Carpenters' greatest hits (me).

One afternoon we paddled the kayak from the beach camp to an island about fifty yards offshore, positive no bears would bother venturing there and we might get some sleep. Moments after stepping ashore, we stood staring at a large, fresh pile of scat.

"I may not be a naturalist, but I know bear shit when I see it," Jennifer said. That's when we resigned ourselves to the fact that Glacier Bay belongs to bears.

Nearly every day we lost or found something. I fumbled a package of flour tortillas overboard and watched as water ballooned into the plastic and sank our only bread to the bottom of the sea. A boat seat went missing, and I perched on a lumpy folded tarp for the rest of the trip. I found a perfectly good Nikon camera behind some bushes where someone had dropped it while peeing. Probably that's what happened, anyway, as it had been quite a few years since bears had killed and eaten kayakers in Glacier Bay. The fact that other people were roaming the backcountry misplacing important items cheered me.

My period started. We chipped at beached icebergs to melt drinking water. Our shoulders ached, and our fingertips grew tender from exposure to brine, rain, and wind. The colder and wearier we became, the more we chafed against each other's personalities. Jennifer's perky "Good morning!" made me want to throw myself in the bay. She called me sullen. I thought her natural bossiness lent her the charisma of a supply sergeant. She suggested that I was too picky about the food. But we were deeply grateful for the companionship of a steady friend, because the most terrible thing of all was to imagine being in this dreadful place alone.

You can read hundreds of accounts by those who journey through Alaska—many inspired by Muir's rapturous prose. People create new versions of such stories all the time, as they become the first, the next, the latest, the oldest, the youngest to scale Denali, walk to the Arctic Ocean, bicycle the Iditarod Trail, hike the Brooks Range, roller skate the Alaska Highway, circumnavigate the Northwest Passage by kayak, dogsled alone to the North Pole. Such adventures sometimes produce what *New York Times Magazine* writer John Tierney famously called "explornography." He defined it as a new genre that "provides vicarious thrills—the titillation of exploring without the risk of actually having to venture into terra incognita." At one time, societies sent out adventurers to extend the world, make it larger. Now we rely on a new kind of adventurer to provide us with hand-me-down experiences, a secondhand life, a virtual high.

For me, it is the old chronicles that are pleasurable because they concern ordinary people who found themselves in an unusual place at an interesting time. There was so much to want, so much to find: a poke of gold, an accurate map, a bit of useful knowledge, a valley to trap, a congregation of believers, a homestead. Some didn't survive, of course. Some died in unheralded, unknown ways. But it's worth remembering that most Alaskans today usually die in distressingly ordinary fashion: traffic accidents, heart attacks, old age. Death waits all around us. So does boredom.

I am especially fond of Lt. Joseph Castner, an army man ordered to search out routes across the territory. Though far from the north's greatest adventurer, in some ways he is among the most valiant for his stubbornness, his earnestness, his sheer ordinariness. For ten months in 1898–99 he trudged from Prince William Sound five hundred miles northward in an attempt to reach Circle City on the Yukon River. He crossed perilous bogs, and rivers heavy with silt, and brush so thick the sky was more idea than reality. It's not clear why his superiors thought this route was important, because others had already mapped and traveled some version of it.

In any case, Castner failed spectacularly, though with a certain stoic dignity. Along the way he and his men ate their mules to keep from starving. They begged supplies from generous Athabascans who themselves struggled daily to live off the country. They tied canvas around their feet to replace their ragged boots. Mosquitoes drained them. Rivers nearly drowned them. The country dragged at them. Every hour's walking was an hour farther from home. But Castner didn't give up until he and his two companions were so hungry that they forced themselves to eat a wolf (tastes like mutton, he reported) and retraced their steps to scavenge the rotting carcass of their dead mule General Jackson. "As my men often said, it would be impossible to make others understand what we suffered those days," he wrote.

Having barely survived this march, the trio gave up on their destination and rafted to the safety of a miner's settlement. When winter arrived, making travel easier, Castner mushed a thousand miles across Alaska and the Yukon so he could report on his failed journey to his superiors. After narrating his ordeal, he concluded by describing Alaska as a "land whose many natural obstacles to travel made this one of the best years of my life."

One of the best years of my life. He meant it. Read the dry narrative of his military report, his faithful assessment of travel and troubles, and you'll see that this statement is the most heartfelt thing he says.

What did he know that I didn't? What did Muir see that I couldn't? All my life I have stood wondering at the edge of impenetrable forests, or flinging rocks across uncrossable rivers, or gazing at the mirage of distant mountains. Why them? Why not you or me?

Sometimes during our trip I could glimpse how quickly trouble would come, not in giant steps, but in small, cumulative lurches toward some invisible threshold. One afternoon, trying to round a point where a nasty chop, roiling currents, and ornery gusts shoved the kayak around, we worried whether we should turn back and camp or blast through a narrow rocky passage toward more sheltered waters. It was the uncertainty that frightened me. Our voices tightened, pinching into anxious registers as we warned each other: *Turn the bow into the waves. Not that way! Paddle hard. Paddle harder!*

As the kayak lumbered through confused seas, I pictured the one treacherous wave that would slop over the side, swamping the boat and pitching us overboard. Then, the struggle to swim ashore through the killing cold, and should we survive that, the futile attempt to find dry matches that had drifted ashore, the trembling efforts to light a fire in the rain with wet wood, the slow surrender to hypothermia on a dark shore, the newspaper headlines about those poor, foolish women . . .

What in God's name were they doing out there anyway, people would wonder.

Jennifer and I never saw Muir Glacier, which had retreated so far up the inlet it was now grinding itself to ice cubes against dry land. With better research we might have known that, but then what would be the point of discovery, of exploration, of journeys undertaken in folly and innocence? We spent two days near Sealers Island waiting for the weather to lift, plodding through the rain to stare at petrified trees, trying to glimpse land otters that denned nearby. I'd worn the wrong kind of raincoat—how quickly the lessons of childhood had deserted me!—and walking around in it was like wearing seaweed. We took gray pictures of each other, in which Jennifer plastered a smile on her face, and I didn't bother to try. "You just look pissed," her husband observed later as he thumbed through our photographs.

The greatest mystery was why I had believed I could fit into this place, how I'd fooled myself into thinking the outdoor life was simple and straightforward, like ordinary life but with thicker socks and more rain gear. All those years I'd considered myself an Alaskan, but in truth I was nearly dismantled, mentally and physically, by this bleak weather and glum landscape, by overwhelming ignorance and uncertainty. I was the navigator George Vancouver gazing unhappily at the coastline he was mapping—shores he described as "uncommonly awful" and "inhospitable" and "horribly magnificent." Not someone who could find providence where others saw only emptiness. Not John Muir, and not the Tlingits either.

We headed back a day early, making a grim fourteen-mile paddle against wind, tide, and rain to catch the ship that transports backcountry travelers. At the pickup point, we discovered that all over the park, kayakers were abandoning their journeys to escape the weather—awful even by Southeast standards—so we didn't feel as bad about fleeing the bay as we might have. The tourists aboard the ship stared at the returning adventurers as if each wet, grubby person were clearly and coincidentally insane.

Finally warm inside and out, Jennifer and I sat in the forward lounge drinking beer. We were a little shell-shocked at the transition—one moment huddling on a cold beach, the next embraced by society's comforts. Everything was so easy! Toilets flushed, heat magicked into being, chairs embraced you. We tacitly forgave each other for the little misunderstandings, cranky exchanges, and put-upon sighs. After a time, Jennifer set down her beer and said, "Now the trip is done, and the story takes over."

And it's true the story has long overwhelmed the experience, that whatever it was I found, most is lost to me except these few small tales, which I have been grinding and polishing ever since, as they are the only riches I discovered.

There is another approach to such journeys, one that I am not taking. This is to seek no attention at all, to refuse any public accounting of your excursions and enlightenments. A friend tells of a man who walked three hundred miles across the Arctic one summer just because it interested him. There are people who regularly travel for weeks by dog team through the Brooks Range or along the frozen plains of the Arctic, simply for the pleasure of traveling through the country in March, the most beautiful of winter months. You will never read their stories. Historian Robert DeArmond, as a teenager in the 1950s, rowed a dory from Sitka to Seattle so he could attend college. He never was interested in writing about what it was like to surf giant rollers and camp each night on the beach. In 1997, a seventy-year-old widower spent three months pulling a sled on a thousand-mile trek from Anchorage to Nome. It was his third such trip. He liked to walk through Alaska in the winter.

One of Alaska's most admired outdoorsmen of contemporary times is Dick Griffith, who finished the brutal Alaska Mountain Wilderness Classic at age seventy-eight in 2004—his seventeenth finish in an overland race across terrain hardly anyone else travels anymore. He has made an incredible number of epic but unpublicized trips throughout Alaska and the Arctic, usually on his own. Griffith once joked in a newspaper story that his only sponsor was the Salvation Army. One winter he skied from Unalakleet along the coast to Barrow, nine hundred miles away. On a different journey, as he traveled near the Mackenzie Delta in Canada, a group of twenty-five Inupiat Eskimos, young and old, suddenly appeared on snowmachines. They towed a sled with a tiny house carrying two elderly women inside. The crowd had been visiting family in Aklavik, Northwest Territories, and was now returning across the imaginary Alaska-Canada border to Kaktovik, two hundred miles away. His encounter reminds us how easily and regularly the Natives and other residents of the Alaska bush travel in the backcountry without the slightest fuss. Griffith finally must have understood their motivation when he wrote in his journal, "The first few years I made lengthy Arctic trips to satisfy my ego. The next few trips were made because I knew I could do better. Now I make Arctic trips because it's that time of year."

A century ago, prospectors and miners crisscrossed the north because they too were headed somewhere, not because they needed to prove anything. T. A. Rickard, who wrote about the Klondike Gold Rush in a 1909 book, observed: "When one hears the true stories of the feats of travel over ice and snow accomplished by the unrecorded heroes of these frontier mining camps, the much advertised expeditions of scientific-newspaper enterprise seem hollow shows." More remarkable and less heralded are stories of Alaska Natives, stories rarely heard about a land most of us would not recognize, much less survive within.

It is not easy to say what anyone can hope to discover in today's world of hollow shows, a world mapped, photographed, described, and experienced within an inch of its life. "So many of us, alas, were born with no Northwest Passage to discover," writes J. Michael Yates. "We spend our lives carrying that poignant absence inside us wherever we go, around and around the earth." Can we help it that we arrived too late, that most of the planet has been all wrapped up and presented to itself with a bow?

I will never climb any mountains, never appear in any record books, never make the cover of *Outside* magazine. I can name a dozen—two dozen!—friends and acquaintances who are stronger, braver, bolder, and more experienced in the outdoors than I'll ever be. At parties I hardly dare trot out some modest tale of excitement or peril. Three other people in the room could trump me with a death-defying excursion they've kept mostly to themselves. Never will I be a professional adventurer or even a half-assed adventurer. At most, I can hope to become an accidental explorer whose only wish is to bust away the maddening, brittle Styrofoam of daily life, to be creative through the simple act of pulling on my boots and walking out the door.

I've told one story of our trip. Here is another:

In Glacier Bay, birdsong floods the meadows each slow dawn like a rising tide.

The cyan sea fills fjords so deep that darkness seems to press against the hull of your boat.

Animals look at you there—harbor seals with eyes luminous in their round skulls, river otters in sharp, quick glances, and, of course, the bears, which you can be quite sure are watching, even when you can't see them.

A porpoise exhales in concussive bursts, but a humpback whale sighs like a slowing calliope.

In my burning heart I learned that I am capable of more than I knew and less than I hoped. It is possible to cross a wave-tossed inlet against the tide and wind if you have no choice, if you deny your body a voice of its own, if you simply bend to the work and think about nothing, because the fact is, you have no choice. Sometimes there is no going back.

Much later I realized it wasn't fear that seized me from time to time on our trip so much as some deeper, painful feeling—the *mysterium tremendum* that comes from a world pressing against flesh, a world that cannot be ignored or mediated or negotiated, a world where constant wind can chafe you, and seeping cold can slow you, and rising seas can swamp you. Still you go on. I tell you, that feeling is something sweet and necessary, no matter how small your journey, no matter how mild. The story that remains is the one thing in this world that belongs only to you. That story is your new home. It is your life.

The Undiscovered Place

EVEN NOW, THE SOUND OF WAVES surging against that shore rises at unexpected moments: as I'm peeling carrots in the kitchen, watching chickadees at the winter feeder, making love with my husband. It's as if I were made of sand, and when the ocean is not washing over me it seeps through me. It holds me together. Sometimes, when everything else quiets, I hear in this inner ocean the sound of something that changes every moment while somehow seeming never to change at all.

I do not know if I will ever return to that place. Going back would not be easy, but it is not impossible. It's the kind of place that draws people, that inhabits stories and is inhabited by them, stories filled with fear and longing, adventure, and mystery.

My friend Hank came on the journey to keep me, or someone like me, from writing about it. He came to keep me from saying its name. Think of the power in that—I could surrender the name right now, and you might look for it on a map, you might search for the few books that name it, you might go there yourself.

But this is not that kind of story, and I am not one of those chroniclers who starts at the beginning and trudges faithfully to an uplifting and satisfying conclusion. Like discovery itself, we expect narrative to start at a particular conjunction of time and place and end in another, persevering from waypoint to waypoint with bearings noted and progress plotted and accomplishments reported. I could march across this page from camp to camp, from night to night, recounting the string of events that loom large in my recollection—the bear on the trail, the calamity at Bad Ass Creek, the solstice party. But where does a wave begin and end? Stories can be like that, too—always breaking over you.

Beneath mountains that burned white like some fevered Renaissance painter's dream, we stripped and leaped into the cold sea. We did it for fun but also to bare ourselves to the world and to each other. There were four of us. For sixty miles we would walk an edge of the continent humming with the steady beat of the Pacific surf. This green verge seems as inviting as a promenade, except for the many creeks and rivers scoring the beach and bold stone headlands jutting seaward. The strand is wide and sandy and sloping, except where it is narrow and rocky and a sailor's dread. The shore is uninhabited, except for a remarkable number of brown bears.

I was there to write about the trip, because that is what I am, a writer who goes places and does things and then writes about it. Mark organized the trip so he could take photographs, because that's how he sees the world. He's a lanky man with black hair and a black beard and eyes that remind you of newly calved glaciers or a certain shade of lupine. He likes to seize what is beautiful in nature and transfer it to the page, but he also believes that nature photographs work best when a person shares the frame.

Mark invited his friend Richard, a former National Park Service ranger who now taught junior high and as a result knew a lot of really terrible jokes. He looks like the kind of dangerous boy you pretended not to like in school but secretly found adorable. He had traveled through this place once before on a difficult trip plagued with poor weather, and this time he meant to have fun. For our first meal he brought a paper bag of buttered popcorn, a dozen fresh bagels, hot sauce, and a Nalgene bottle sloshing with margaritas.

Hank was there to stop us. He was born and reared in Alaska, and he'd retired from the National Park Service at the age of thirty to master something unusual, which is the art of doing what he wants and not much else. Hank's gravelly voice is completely at odds with the freshness of his passion and an earnestness that makes a person question her own cynical, squint-eyed view of life. He's six feet tall and sturdy, and a decade or more younger than the rest of us. His hair and beard are ginger-colored and beyond control, and if you say something to him about it he will lift his hand to his head as if suddenly discovering a wild animal has taken up lodging on his skull.

After he heard about Mark's plans to publish photographs and words about this place, Hank began strafing us with e-mails and phone calls. First he tried to talk Mark out of the trip. Then he convinced Mark to bring him along while trying to persuade Mark to leave his cameras behind. "It may change the way you see the place," he wrote. Finally he attempted to inspire us to higher levels of thought and conscience by sending us messages with statements like "Every time a recreational experience is made accessible another experience goes extinct in its wake." He fretted about the impossibility of balancing the "voice of preservation with the come-see-it response of a book broadcasting the beauty of the place."

Hank's opposition sprang from the certainty that as soon as people discover a place that can be described as untouched, wild, dangerous, beautiful, pristine, secret, or unique, it's doomed. He gave examples. Denali National Park, he said, is a "zoo without bars" where habituated bears walk freely around tour buses instead of running away from them as sensible bears should. He regards most of Glacier Bay National Park as a damaged paradise, a scenic purgatory where kayakers and cruise boat passengers alike feel smug about their lack of environmental effect while actually changing the way bears and whales and other creatures behave.

I did not know what to make of Hank. Who among us does not have a favorite spot we want to hide? But those who argue for wilderness preservation usually mean preservation from everyone but themselves. And to insist that humans don't belong in wilderness at all only widens the chasm between people and nature, separating us from a sense of belonging to the world. Without that connection, how can we care for it properly?

Then I spent a night at Hank's cabin while we waited for our hiking companions to arrive. He lives in what he calls "a small house by a small stream in a small town." Here's how Richard describes Hank's life: "Walk barefoot. Build your own cabin. Give massages. Grow your own food. Women love that shit. Bastard."

We steamed in a sauna Hank had built in the spruce forest and then cooled ourselves in the clear creek running alongside. For dinner we ate things he had killed and gathered and grown and made: venison and garden vegetables and berry liqueurs. We talked about wilderness and loss, and whether there was any way to separate the two. And by the next day, when we climbed aboard a floatplane to begin our journey, I'd begun wondering why I was writing about this trip, and who I was writing it for.

We did not walk alone. Our steps followed three bear trails that will exist as long as there are bears. The first appears as bears amble along the beach, their massive paws plowing up the sand and sometimes leaving perfect imprints. After a time, you no longer bother to bend and place a hand inside these tracks for a cheap thrill. Hank stepped inside one hind print; he wears size 13 boots, and both of his feet fit neatly within the outline. It was easy to imagine bears wandering pigeon-toed along the shore, nosing at dead fish and debris, squatting now and then, lifting their muzzles to sniff the news of the ocean. Once in a while I raised my head from the mesmerizing prints in case the maker was a dark shape just beyond.

Sometimes the scuff of prints moves away from the ocean toward the forest. Above the tidal margin a meadow grows, thick with ryegrass, purple lupines, wild iris, beach pea. The bears walk a second trail through these high meadows—digging up roots, munching on grasses, nibbling berries—and their tread wears the vegetation into mud.

The third bear trail runs through the forest, just inside the trees. Sometimes this route is as wide and well cleared as if a trail crew had brushed it out. In places you can step from one plate-sized depression to another, as evenly spaced as stepping-stones, though you will need to stretch your gait uncomfortably to catch the rhythm. Now and then you must crawl under tree limbs, pressing your face close to the earth and recalling that bears do not walk on their rear legs, that they see and smell the world mostly from this elevation. Occasionally a promising route turns unaccountably inland and then fades, leaving you standing in green shadows, wondering which way to go.

We saw the first bear within two hours of our start. First we came upon its piss dribbled across the stones. Ahead a bulky shape nosed among the boulders, no doubt searching for what the sea had left. The brown bear vanished into the trees before we caught up.

The second bear surprised us later that day along a forest path. Mark and I heard whistle blasts and yelling, and we hurried toward the others. "That was a big bear," Richard was saying as we ran up. The bear had been moseying along the trail when everyone surprised each other. Richard blasted his whistle, and the bear wheeled and galloped back the way it came. Richard guessed it weighed seven hundred pounds.

Hank hung back as we started walking again. "Dang, I hate to scare bears," he said. I nodded, although I was relieved the bear had run away. It didn't have to.

"Maybe it's better if that's their reaction to hunters," I offered.

That night, Hank was still thinking about it. "What would make that bear turn and run from us today?" he asked. "He weighed more than all four of us together. Why would he be scared?"

It was hard for me to imagine being so close to a bear and feeling anything but fear, but that's not how Hank thought. Once he described following big tracks during his first trip here. After a couple of miles the tracks left the beach and moved up into the grass. That's where Hank found the bear, lying in the rich, aromatic grass with its chin propped on a log. It rolled over on its back with its paws in the air and rolled back, a creature at complete ease in its world. It never saw Hank, who crept away and has wished ever since that he had stayed and watched.

You can buy a map of Alaska that is nothing but a dream suitable for framing, a beautiful lie that shows the entire state as landscape unmarked, unnamed, untouched. But walk for a bit, anywhere you choose, and you must surrender that lovely falsehood. So many have been here before us—the Indian and Eskimo nations, of course—and everyone who came later has somehow marked the place, scored it, measured it, described it.

The first people who lived along this shore say that old trickster Raven was busy in these provinces, and their names identify the sites where he landed his kayak and built his house and opened the box of daylight that illuminated the world. The original names resonate in a tongue rarely spoken. Every day we walked at the feet of cloud-catchers, glacier-makers, perpetual beacons for those far at sea. On the tallest of these peaks a stone refuge was built during High Tide All Around, which we remember as The Flood. The fact that we don't all know the stories does not mean these events did not occur.

The Russians left their own names and brass markers and sometimes men behind. The Europeans, always nuzzling along the shores searching for their beloved passages north, their shortcuts to glory, surveyed some coastlines inch by inch. They found the mountains forbidding and the forests gloomy, yet still they gilded everything with the names of honoraries and family members who would never once look upon this land.

All through the years the coast has borne shipwrecks and whaling stations, trading posts and anchorages, canneries and lighthouses, mines carved into mountains and fox farms crouched among the trees. We passed places where men were once shot or hanged, mining machinery abandoned, and boats left to rot upon the shore. But mostly what we saw were the modern reminders of a civilization somewhere nearby: derelict crab pots catching only sand and grass, coils of net and fishing line, detergent bottles with Korean labels, empty five-gallon plastic buckets. The yellow buckets, Hank pointed out, were punctured on the corners by bears mysteriously attracted to "yum-yum yellow."

So common were bear tracks that it was a shock to see two fading sets of human footprints along the beach, one large, one small. We named their owners Frank and Lulu. Tire tracks marked the sand now and then, and Hank told us that pilots were landing tourists here to picnic by the sea.

"Look at the globe," he said. "You can't sharpen your pencil sharp enough to color in this part of the coastline, it's so small." Yet people were finding their way here.

One afternoon a scrap of blue seized my eye among a driftwood tangle. I reached for a plastic turtle no larger than my palm. It was one of twenty-nine thousand bathtub toys lost from a barge container that capsized far out to sea in 1992. I stashed the turtle away like a treasure from a foreign land. A day later I lost it in the forest, and I like to think of that innocent mariner growing moss among the trees.

At one of our camps Hank disappeared and returned with a strange glass device as large as a medicine ball. He'd stashed it away on his last hike, having no way to carry it home and no reason to leave it to the tide. It must have been some kind of meteorological instrument, but out here it seemed like wizardry, an indecipherable message from a strange and distant land, something we could not decide whether to save or to smash.

Should you ever find this place, here are some things you ought to know:

Expect the surf to thrum along the shore so insistently that it vibrates in your flesh, your bones, your blood. A perpetual mist lies ahead and behind, an exhalation of waves, until finally you realize you are walking through this briny aerosol every moment.

Beyond the strand the forest waits, dim and cool. Step inside, keep going, and you could cross the continent to the Atlantic Ocean.

In a certain cove the waves break just right and fur seals surf long, glassy combers. Envy them for a moment before you hoist your heavy pack and trudge forward again, you cursed landlubber, you forlorn traveler.

When you reach the beach where tiny gray crabs lie mired in the sand, toss some back in the water. Screw Darwin.

Later you'll see a beach purple with crushed mussel shells. Walk in indigo.

Find the beach where the sea spends a few hours every day smoothing and polishing fat boulders of green and gray and granite. You could live here, making your bed in a different stone hollow every night with the tide washing all around you.

In the twilight, listen to the ocean folding upon the shore, over and over, and think of all the ways it carries sound—ringing like a struck bell with the melodies of whales, hissing with the mutterings of fish, chanting in the wind like a Greek monody. A wave that began in the Sea of Japan will fall at your feet and unleash the tones of all these things, and more.

You cannot lose your way. Remember to follow the sea, though it planes toward a horizon with no sharp edge, no curve, but only a blank restlessness to show where sky and water smudge.

We carried our own histories, our own bits of flotsam and jetsam. At dawn, birdsong cascaded over us, and when the sun warmed the tent Hank would say dreamily, "Hit me with a poem," and I'd read something from a book by Mary Oliver.

As we sat around the driftwood fire drinking coffee and eating oatmeal and watching the sea, Richard would recite something particularly vile from the book he'd brought—*Women*, by Charles Bukowski—and we would laugh ourselves silly, don't ask me why, with Richard pointing at us and saying, "Funny, ain't it? That counts, right?" He was our own trickster, constantly reminding us of our humanity. If Hank wanted to point out what was sacred in nature, we could count on Richard to make us laugh at the profane.

On the only rainy day (and wasn't *that* a miracle, the lack of rain?) our man-made tools failed us: first the gas stove we needed for coffee, and then the lighter that would not spark, and then the knife blade that snapped as we dug pitch from a tree trunk, and finally that sorry fire itself, which refused to do anything but smolder sullenly in the wet duff. Only because the rain stopped did our humiliations cease.

Of course, we were here not just to experience the coast but also to document it somehow, to understand it as best we could. Mark carried twenty-five pounds of camera gear and looked around with measuring eyes. Sometimes he rose at 4 a.m. to photograph flowers in that dewy light that lends every streak of grass, every petal and pistil, every bud and hollow the radiance of its own particular existence. The mountains—they were just the same in that light, a shattered geometry of snow and stone made translucent against the sky.

And me, with my notebooks and pencils always ready for some detail, some scribbled comment, some insight. What a burden longing was—to stand on the continent's soft edge, waves always and endlessly arriving, the surf breathing for you, and that old, old dream of paradise stirring deep, as if it were a place you could locate, a place where you could never stay but would instead spend the rest of your life yearning to return to. A place like this.

Heavier still was the weight of not knowing what to do. I am a writer, so what else could I do but scrawl into those notebooks? What else can I do but tell you what I saw? To keep this place hidden, to pretend it does not exist, or better yet, that it exists beyond our capacity to discover its true meaning—there was a burden I did not know if I could carry.

The capes beat us up but good. Boulders the size of two-room apartments crowded the points, so we climbed into the woods. Sometimes we jujitsued our way through alder thickets, which Hank called "pucker brush" because of the way your face screws up in a weak attempt to protect itself as you thrust through the maddening tangle. You can't save yourself. You just have to wave your arms wildly and take it.

Inside the forest we were thrashed soundly by thorny devil's club, rotting logs, perilous slopes. The rain forest perched on a green skin of moss fuzzing the jumble of boulders, and sometimes without notice a misstep plunged our legs into dank gaps between stone.

Sweating, cursing, bug-bit, and slashed, we emerged into a giant tangle of old driftwood. We teetered along the slippery

wood, packs pulling us off balance, jagged branches threatening to impale us. Mark called me a "candy-ass" once when I
hollered for help. Desperate for drinking water, we filled our
bottles from a pool sluggish with algae. We had left the water
filter behind to save weight, so I banished thoughts of high
school experiments involving protozoa and gulped.

One night, submissive and aching, we camped two feet
from a muddy bear trail, sleeping on a bed of wild strawberries, moss, and chocolate lilies as rain pitty-patted on the tents.
We'd traveled perhaps eight miles.

"A cakewalk," Hank had said.

Early on the summer solstice we stopped to camp and observe
pagan rituals. First we built a bonfire next to a placid creek.
Hank scavenged a five-gallon bucket that bears hadn't punctured, and we heated rocks at the fire's edge and dropped them
steaming into the water. Mark and Richard wandered off so I
could bathe and Hank turned his back to tend the fire. To feel
the warmness coursing over my skin as I stood naked to the
world—it seemed elemental, sanctifying.

Later Richard claimed he hadn't actually been peeking at
me through the binoculars but rather had been checking to
see if Hank was peeking. By then it didn't matter. We had all
stripped so many times to cross deep creeks or splash in the
ocean that we had few secrets left.

We could not stop talking as we walked or sat around the
fire at night, telling stories about the misjudgments and hopes
of youth, the calculations and satisfactions of middle age. All
of us had partners. All of us had other lives that had little

to do with this one, but those people, those worries, seemed dreamy and remote. Hank said he and a good friend had often wondered at how easily people open to each other on such trips. But on returning to civilization most people shutter themselves inside again. How could a person stop himself from doing that?

Probably that's why he spoke so candidly about what he wanted as we stood around the fire, clean and warm and full of instant cheesecake. Hank argued that this shoreline deserves protection from everybody, not just from pilots, and drop-in tourists, and hunters, but from wanderers like us.

"It's a subtle thing, because we're not killing bears," he said. "But we're changing it, just a little. Somewhere ahead of us, bears are moving aside. How long before they stop?"

It was arrogant to seek new restrictions, he said, and he himself didn't want more regulations, but he could not foresee other choices. "It's the only coast that even has a small chance of being saved," he said. "In a roundabout way, it asks the question, just because we can go to a place, should we?"

But how, Mark wondered, could this place be shielded from people? Hank had thought that through, too.

"Imagine fifty years from now where only six parties can go on a stretch of wild beach, and they become the storytellers, and everyone else has to accept it as a vicarious experience," he said. "That's my vision. That's my dream. But you know how damn radical that is."

Something twisted inside me at this idea. I could not imagine never returning here. Would someone else's story satisfy?

Waves began sloshing over the spit, dislodging a flock of complaining seagulls. It occurred to us to check the tide book:

an 11.6-foot tide was on its way, the highest of the month. A tidal bore surged up the creek toward the bonfire. The ocean slipped among the coals, extinguishing them in steamy gouts, but the logs suspended above continued blazing among the waves.

A mist followed the tide ashore. Hank and I walked in bare feet along the sand. Every artifact that appeared glowed in the mysterious light: crab claws, mussel shells, razor clams, eagle feathers, wolf prints that paced along the water before disappearing into the sea. Fresh bear prints dropped from the meadow and headed toward the water's edge. We sat against the cut bank, imagining the bear stepping off the ledge over our heads and then lumbering into the silvery mist, giving us no notice at all.

But that's not the way it works. We were following Frank and Lulu's footsteps along the coast. Ahead of us, bears were slipping into the woods as those two people passed. Bears were turning to see us coming in our own bubble of noise and scent.

"What if you knew this was the last time you'd see this?" I asked. "Would you give that up in exchange for more regulations?"

"Joyfully," Hank said.

In the afternoons we slept on the beach, curled into sandy hollows or against logs, like any other tired creature. One day we stripped and jumped in the ocean and then draped ourselves across smooth boulders to dry in the sun.

I closed my eyes to memorize the sound of the ocean: rising to meet us, slipping away, rising, retreating. It was the pause between waves that held me, the caesura, the promise. Then we put our clothes back on and hoisted our packs and walked, skittering along the shore like sandpipers to avoid the foaming surf. The ocean soaked into the sand, unsettling every grain, and then seeped away, leaving the ground firm again.

At night I slept as well as I ever have, which was odd considering I had never seen so much bear sign in my life. In the mornings we rose late, our inner clocks cranking us around so that we did what we wanted when we wanted. At 10 p.m. we ate dinner, then 11 p.m., then midnight.

Mark framed pictures in his mind and then in his camera. He weighed light, he judged angles, he peered through his lens just as the original inhabitants had stared at European ships through twisted leaves of skunk cabbage. For all that he had teased Hank, he now worried about the problem of portraying this place in print. How could he not share pictures of such startling beauty? Couldn't making people understand this place help Hank rally support, at least for eliminating plane landings along the coast? Early in the trip Mark and I had tried to coax Hank into letting us write about him and his cause, but Hank was horrified at the prospect of appearing in a glossy national magazine. He knew plenty of people would ignore the words, be seduced by the photographs, and undertake their own hikes here.

Such things have happened before. When a Canadian company began making plans to build a giant copper mine near the Tatshenshini River in the wilderness of British Columbia, the environmental outcry was such that thousands of people immediately signed up for raft trips so they could see what the hoopla was about. They forced land managers on both sides of the border to create a permit system to keep all those river-lovers from ruining what they longed to save. And even now, how many among us who are outraged and heartbroken over the potential fate of the Arctic National Wildlife Refuge cannot wait to take ourselves to that plain, just so we can love the place in person?

Before we reached Bad Ass Creek we had no trouble crossing streams and creeks and sloughs. We waded through shallow waters cursing and whooping at the way the cold numbed our feet and made our stomachs hurt. "Damn, I hate glacial water," Richard would say every time. We coveted the insulation of Hank's neoprene booties; he wore them because once he had ripped a toenail off during a stream crossing without feeling it, the water was so cold.

For deeper waters, we unpacked two tiny one-man rafts, inflated them and paddled over, feet dangling out the front. Two people would cross, one would return towing an empty raft, and so on. The pack rafts were a clever solution, but they were not what you would call sturdy, with their midget paddles and uncertain equilibrium. One of them popped a D-ring seal the first time we used it, which Hank and Richard fixed with duct tape.

On the map Bad Ass Creek was a spidery blue line. In real life it was more like a river, thirty yards wide, glacial-fed and unruly as it poured into the ocean surf. For a couple of hours we tried to figure out how to cross. Hank and Mark led the way up and down the banks, searching for a shallow spot or a convenient log.

Richard told the story of a guy named Steve who years before had led a group of young, inexperienced people along the coast. While crossing this creek wearing only underwear and no shoes, he'd been washed downstream. He climbed out on the opposite bank, almost naked and certainly freezing. Night fell. In bare feet, he thrashed his way in the dark along the riverbank until finally he found a logjam to cross over. When he staggered into camp, feet shredded, his arrival was regarded as miraculous.

"They did call him Suicide Steve after that," Richard added.

We discussed our choices. Mark asked me what I wanted to do, but I could not say. I was afraid to wade across that powerful, freezing water and equally afraid to paddle the rushing current. Finally they inflated the boats, tied a line around Hank's waist, and stashed a set of clothes, a lighter, and a knife in a dry bag for him to take. I offered him my plastic emergency signal card, which was covered with hieroglyphic figures waving their arms about in cryptic motions that meant help, food, rescue.

"Let's get our signals straight," he said. "Two 'Oh, shits' means I'm in trouble. One 'Oh, fuck' equals three 'Oh, shits.'"

Hank kneeled in the raft and launched himself across the milky river, paddling madly. The boat rocked and the current pulled it downstream. We held our breath as he deftly maneuvered the paddle until he reached the other shore.

"No problem," he shouted with an encouraging wave. Mark and Richard pulled the raft back along the thin line now stretching across the river.

My turn. Richard and Mark tied me to the raft with a rope around my waist. "Pull this toggle if something happens and you need to let go of the raft," Richard said, waggling a short stick looped into the line.

They steadied the raft in an eddy behind a log's upturned roots. The rubber craft seemed impossibly small. "My daughter has a swimming pool bigger than that," Richard said later. "Why didn't we just bring that? It's cheaper, too. With duckies on it."

I eyed the raft before climbing in. "Should I kneel or sit?"

"Kneel," they agreed, handing me the paddle as I tried to balance.

I began paddling inexpertly, pulling the boat out of their hands.

"No, sit!" one of them shouted, seeing what I did not yet understand.

As soon as the raft hit the main current, I felt it shift. Such moments have an inevitability about them. That's how I felt as the boat flipped, anyway. I recognized that I was meant to fall in the river, and I surrendered to it.

Instant immersion into shocking cold. The raft covered my head. Vaguely I heard shouting. Water filled my boots, and my feet dragged along the bottom. I don't know if I pushed the raft away or the river did, but now it was floating behind me. I tried to stand, but the rope yoking me to the raft tightened and yanked me off my feet.

Oh, I was angry. How humiliating to be the one to lose control, to be the woman who fell in the river and lost the boat. There was no room for fear with an anger that size.

Turn your feet downstream, I remembered from other raft trips, and I floated around to face the sea. If I didn't reach the shore soon the river would carry me into the surf, and that was not a good place to be, pounded by seven-foot waves against rocks and sand.

The raft floated free. That was good, because I never would have remembered to pull the toggle. But that was bad, because we needed both rafts. The river dragged me along, and I scraped against the bottom until I washed up against a gravel bar about one hundred yards downstream from the launch site.

The men were running and shouting along the shore. Hank splashed through a channel until he reached me. Richard chased the boat toward the sea. We could not lose that raft or we would have trouble crossing upcoming streams—or this one, for that matter.

"Are you okay?" Hank asked, helping me ashore.

"C-c-cold." I was so cold. Never had I been this cold.

"The b-b-boat," I said.

"We'll get it," he said. "I'm going after it. Go build a fire."

But my fury at myself was the only thing that could warm me, and I trudged toward the ocean to help. A small tributary stopped me. I was shaking so hard I could not make myself wade through more cold water, and I could not keep my balance on a log, and so I turned back to find the dry bag and change, and try, hands trembling, to make a fire.

I heard shouting and there was Richard, triumphantly lofting the raft above his head. Hank returned and helped with the fire as I jumped up and down for warmth. He told me the truth about his own crossing: "All the way over I was saying, 'Oh fuck, oh fuck, oh fuck.' And then on the other side I said, 'It's fine! No problem!'" I felt better.

On the other side, Richard mooned me to cheer me up.

"It's more fun when you live!" he shouted.

I could hardly pay attention as the men hollered and signaled and finally worked out a system to reunite us all on one
side of the river. One by one, Hank pulled the packs over and
sent the raft back. Mark fell to the ground and crossed himself
as his camera gear crept over. Then he and Richard crossed, one
at a time. They did not bother trying to paddle but instead
crouched to lower the raft's center of gravity.

When we were all together, we ate macaroni and cheese and
told our parts of the story, laughing and shouting and talking
over each other. "When you live, you babble. When you die,
you're very, very quiet," Richard said.

He pointed out that Hank may have seemed like the hero
for pulling me out of the water, but he, Richard, had saved the
boat and thus the expedition. He had faced a moral dilemma, he
explained, because his favorite hat had flown off as he ran along
the shore. Should he save the woman, the raft, or the hat?

We quieted when someone spotted a bear poking along
the shore, head down and silhouetted against the horizon.
Instinctively we moved together. It did not see us. When it
reached the broad stream, it walked into the water and paddled
calmly through the deepness until it reached the other side,
climbed out, shook itself, and kept walking.

We looked around at all of our gear strewn about, at the
macaroni and cheese, the cameras and packs, my clothes drying
by the fire. It had taken us four hours to cross that river, hours
filled with planning and consternation and shouting and fear.
The bear had accomplished the same thing in perhaps three
minutes. A greater demonstration of human frailty I could
not imagine.

In the night, or what passes for it, a bear approached our tents. Its tracks circled around a place in the sand where someone had pissed and then turned back. We never heard it. Dazed by the sun's heat, we slept late and then dawdled around camp, complaining about our aches, telling stories that maybe we hadn't told anybody in a long time.

That day I felt like I could walk forever with those three men. I had fallen in love, not with them but with something in each of them: their strength, their humor, their confidence, and the way they had given themselves to this place. We could walk and walk. We could eat beach greens and fish, jump in the ocean, talk through the nights. What could stop us?

At last we packed up and left. Far behind us, the promontory dissolved in sea mist, and ahead miles of beach sloped toward the sea. The mountains followed like waves, always breaking toward us. At 3:30 p.m., after walking for only ninety minutes, we stopped for lunch and studied the map: thirteen miles to the place where a plane would retrieve us the next afternoon. Sure had a lot of mileage to make up. Better get a move on. Time to start hustling.

"Let's take a nap," someone suggested, so we did. It was the last chance we'd have to sleep unawares on the beach.

At 5 p.m., yawning and dopey, we heaved our packs onto our shoulders and marched steadily, stopping once an hour. The sun burned our faces. We walked apart. The sea slid toward us, away, toward us, away, foam hissing and bubbling and sweeping in great lacy arcs across the sand. We did not stop to watch a half-dozen eagles eating small fish on a sand-bar. We walked like people who had to be somewhere.

Five hours later, Richard and Hank climbed a grass-covered sand dune to see where we were. Hank turned and thrust his thumb up, and Mark and I followed them over the rise into a wide field of beach rye glowing in the late sun. The light played around the silhouettes of Richard and Hank as they waded through the grass toward a tidal slough. Beyond them was a river delta where people have long fished for salmon. On the other side of the slough, two boys climbed a pole to have a look at us. Shacks, skiffs, drying racks, and other signs of fish camps were scattered through the grass and alders.

Hank scuffed at the mud and walked away, head down.

"Hank's sad," Mark said kindly.

Me, too. Until that moment, I hadn't realized our hike was over. We never paused at the shore to watch the sea for a time, to look back at how far we'd come, to say something overly solemn and then make jokes. I felt tricked.

We blew up the rafts. Hank and I paddled across the slough first. We stopped in the middle to complain. What was our hurry? Why were we rushing toward the end? How could it be over? "Goddammit," Hank said.

Tonight we'd sit late by the fire until the sky grew as dark as it ever does that time of year. A mangy red fox would creep out of the shadows, sniffing and curious and looking for an easy meal. Hank would stand motionless in the tall grass as the fox came closer and closer, and Richard would lean over and mutter into my ear, "The Fox Whisperer," and we would stifle snorts of laughter. It would be a perfect, sad night, because just across the slough and over the grassy rise the Pacific Ocean would continue falling onto the land, each wave completing something made hundreds of miles away. In the morning we would eat wild strawberries and wash ourselves in clean water. Mark and Richard would buy fresh whole salmon from a fisherman. A man would tell Hank and me that our arrival had boosted the number of travelers along the shore that season to eighteen.

Eighteen, he said, was already twice as many people as the year before.

But that night, I listened to the muffled sound of the distant surf fluttering against the tent and wondered if I would ever walk this coast again.

Now, whenever winter stills me, I break its hold by imagining not just a week, or a month, but some shapeless piece of time spent living there, time enough that I might sleep night after night in the same meadow, waiting for that bear to come walking out of the mist along the shore, hoping to see the wolf that paces by the sea.

I have written this story over and over again. Every draft was like a map. In the early versions I named my fool head off. I wanted readers to fall in love with this place, to long to see it. I wanted you to think, *She went there, so why not me?* I figured you'd believe, as I did once, that humans belong in all wild places. I assumed that you, like me, are careful with fire and trash and eager to behave like responsible citizens of a tender world. You would ask: *Don't we all deserve to share in such experiences, to feel wonder and fear and delight, to go where other people don't?*

Yes, I would tell you. And also: No.

Because even though the place we went is not the purest kind of wilderness, it's something very close to what we imagine wilderness to be. I don't know how else we can keep such places from becoming another Denali or Glacier Bay or Yellowstone, except by deciding, each of us on our own, not to go there. That's what Hank said: *Just because we can go to a place, should we?*

Unless you say no to yourself now and then, you will not know what's worth surrendering. You will not accept that a person walking along a beach has the power to change the way a bear lives, unless you relinquish that power.

At first I believed that writing with passion, making a direct appeal to readers, would work. Another writer, who has on occasion kept the names of places to himself, told me that when places are endangered, it's better to build a constituency, better to share knowledge and hope for the best.

Better to have faith in people to do the proper thing, is what he means.

Hank and others agreed that advice sounds well balanced and fair and reasonable. They begged me not to name the place anyway. They don't trust me, and they don't trust you, and I think they might be right about all of us.

As I write this, and as you read it, waves curl against the shore. The earth shifts, trees fall, glaciers retreat, and the ocean . . . the ocean. If the bears have been seized by winter, if they are not this very moment rambling along that slight margin between the dark forest and the darker sea, then soon they will be.

But you and I know nothing remains the same. How, then, would we stop the eighteen from becoming eighty, and eight hundred, and eight thousand? How should we conspire to erase this smallest place from the globe? How can we give it back to Raven and declare it the undiscovered country?

That is a question I don't even know how to answer for myself.

You may find this place, or another like it, all on your own. No one can stop you—not me, not the rivers, not the weather or the bears. But first, ask yourself: Can this story be enough for you? Are you content to be a listener, or must you be a storyteller, too?

Impedimenta

ONCE I RAFTED THE COPPER RIVER with a woman prepared for almost anything that can happen in the wilderness:
bug bites, bear attacks, uncomfortable campsites, nicotine fits,
broken spectacles, flesh wounds, tooth decay. Kari Barnard is
a stout Viking of a woman with flaxen hair, rosy cheeks, and
merry blue eyes. She looks as if she can belt out arias, which
she can, having trained for the opera early in life. Instead
of wearing a horned helmet and singing Wagner, she taught
music to schoolchildren in Gakona, a town near the Wrangell
Mountains. She is a third-generation Alaskan who at that
time lived with a malamute in a crooked old log cabin painted
carmine. Because she suffers from attention deficit disorder,
throughout her cabin she affixed to mirrors and drawers and

cupboards dozens of notes penciled with reminders of what she should do next. She is a woman intent on preventing life from catching her unawares.

Kari and I were among a dozen teachers and writers floating the river's upper section. A century ago, Ahtna Athabascans, explorers, and prospectors traveled the muscular Copper River because it offered a natural cleft into the interior of Alaska. No one can say how many people have been lost over the decades to the river's lower rapids or to the wilds surrounding it. This is a place where it's best to know what you're doing, where you would want the proper gear.

For most of us, camping means going without, making do. Not for Kari. Every night, as the rest of us scrambled into angular cocoons made of space-age fabrics, Kari grandly entered an old-fashioned tent bold and palatial enough to stand up inside. She slept on a queen-size air mattress. She spread a self-inflating pad across the floor for cushioning and covered it with an orange-yellow rug for hominess. A flashlight dangled from the roof so she could read, perhaps while relaxing in the special chair she had brought, a clever contraption that unfolded to provide sturdiness, comfort, and armrests. It was her occasional pleasure while camping to sit outside naked enjoying a cigarette and the night air.

River rafting tolerates far more gear than backpacking, so most people do bring along a few minor amenities—an old guitar, say, or a fifth of whiskey. (I myself would not have dreamed of leaving behind my little pillow.) Kari, however, was a walking 7-Eleven of the wilderness. Wherever she went, she carried a massive hip pack into which she had stuffed dental floss and a dental floss holder, antibacterial ointment, a Gas-X pill in its plastic blister, Pepto-Bismol tablets, eyedrops, tooth-paste. She'd brought a mouth-to-mouth resuscitation shield, a pressure bandage, and latex gloves crammed into a film canister "in case you have to handle anyone's blood," she said.

She pulled out matches, a small notebook, fingernail clip-pers, chocolate-peanut-butter protein bars, and a lens-cleaning cloth in case she lost her contacts and needed to polish her glasses. Also: extra batteries, tampons, carabiners, film, Ritalin pills, a miniature screwdriver, a Phillips screwdriver, a camera, and a tube of Vagisil ointment to ease the itch and pain from mosquito bites, thus making bug repellent unnecessary.

In a special emergency kit she'd tucked away a Band-Aid, a ten-dollar bill, a couple of quarters, gum, and a spare set of nail clippers, should she lose the other pair. She displayed a crimped pack of cigarettes "for those reverent moments when you need to have total sensory overload," she said. Finally she unfolded a fuzzy wad that with a flick of her wrist transformed into a set of earmuffs: "They're small, compact, and instantly on your head," she said, demonstrating with the aplomb of a flight attendant. "And instantly off."

A compact umbrella dangled from the hip belt. Kari's theory was that, abruptly unfolded, the umbrella would startle the average bear into retreat. I thought she could probably just clobber the bear into submission with the pack.

My own survival kit is spare. It consists of a sealed can the size of a large tin of tuna fish. Inside (as best I remember) is a packet of sugar, a length of twine, a few matches, and some chicken bouillon. The can doubles as a cooking container. Outside the can I've wrapped several layers of duct tape, believ-ing, like any good Alaskan, there is almost no situation that duct tape cannot remedy. So far it has acted more as a talisman than a lifesaver. The day I open it is the day I'm in trouble.

After Kari showed me her gear, I began fretting that with my smug little can, I was just asking for trouble. After all, what you take into the wilderness defines not just your intentions, but you. One guideline—the one Kari follows—is to prepare for any possibility, however remote. Another is to hope that what you can do—what you know—is far more important than what you can carry, because you can only carry so much.

These principles could apply to every part of your life, but when traveling through the wilderness, hoisting everything important on your back, you feel the plain, heavy reconciliation between trusting your things and trusting yourself. How do you know what you can do without? Only by doing without.

Years ago my husband and I lost nearly everything we owned in an uninsured fire. We had been together nearly ten years, and what burned up included the ordinary encumbrances of anyone's life: dishes, bookcases, a computer, my wedding dress, notes on the refrigerator, a brand-new reading chair. Most of what was consumed by flames or ruined by water no longer comes to mind, though I regret losing a boxed compilation of Bruce Springsteen albums I had just received for Christmas, and a mastodon tooth given me years before by a friend.

Before the fire, my husband and I did not consider ourselves particularly well-off, though we did not realize how much we had owned until it came time to replace things, a process that took years. Now sometimes I look around my crowded house and wonder if fires every ten years or so aren't rather cleansing, as they are with forests—clearing away the underbrush, renewing the impulse and vigor of life and its possibilities.

Some things were, of course, truly irreplaceable: our three cats, for instance, or the scores of old books recently sent by my great-aunt, who was deeding me her treasured library of classics and first editions. For a long time I could not shake the notion that all those words had cindered into the January sky like tiny keening voices.

Somehow, remarkably, I had lived well into my twenties without understanding that life does not owe you anything, that good fortune can disappear in a flicker, that so much of daily living is staged with elaborate props, most of them only temporary. Now I knew how profoundly untrustworthy the universe could be.

There was gratitude as well. Only a fool wouldn't be thankful for what persisted: our lives, our generous friends, our marriage. But sometimes I think of those vanished belongings with an ache that mimics the ghostly echo of a lost limb. It's not the object itself that causes such twinges, but rather the feeling about it, the faint and yearning recollection of things I once needed that tantalizes and perplexes, again and again.

In 1898–99, Lt. Joseph Castner walked five hundred miles from the southern coast of Alaska to the Tanana River. By the end of his trek, having outwalked and outlived several mules, he had nothing good to say about backpacking. "The least desirable form of transportation for man is the earliest," he wrote, "loading his worldly goods on his own back."

The word used for gear then was "impedimenta." The things that hinder progress. Which things those are, though, we almost never recognize at the time we pack them.

Thus Frederick Cook, phony conqueror of Denali, would not relinquish two big boxes of aneroids, theodolites, and other scientific instruments, despite the peevish hints of his chronicler, Robert Dunn, who knew how the packhorses would suffer under such burdens.

"The professor fusses, fusses, fusses with his instruments, which he carries in two big boxes, that will make trouble when we begin to pack everything," Dunn wrote in *The Shameless Diary of an Explorer*. "He opens a plush case, peeks in, wipes off the brass, closes case again—and there you are. That's hitting the trail real hard. That's scientific exploration."

But then Dunn was a man who thought nearly every item brought by others was misguided or vain. He used a companion's botanizing tin to store cooked beans. He applauded the loss of the poor fellow's mosquito head net: "They blind and deafen, and if a man as God made him can't stand the 'skeets, he's no right up in this country." He scorned outfitting: "I hate it—lists of grub, clothing, saddlery, pots; musing on how neatly this new poncho buckle will free your arm, that cheese-cloth lining make your tent mosquito-proof. We clicked and condemned each neat, new, folding device that will not last a minute on the tundra."

I like to imagine Dunn shaking his head as he flips through an REI catalog or pages through Campmor's, my favorite Compendium of Things You Probably Don't Need. Most everything seems a recapitulation of daily life: espresso makers, portable showers, spice kits. What would he make of the three-person folding camp couch, the inflatable sink, the Luggable Loo?

Unlike Dunn, I adore outfitting. In daily life, I am unfocused, sloppy, and excessive, but give me a backpack and a pile of gear, or a kayak and a heap of dry bags, and I can lose myself in organizing, itemizing, and packing. Almost no situation cannot be soothed by a list. I make dozens of them, just so I can check things off. A person like me needs such boundaries. What can fit in a boat, what can be hefted in a pack—that and no more.

Always, one dry bag won't quite wedge into the bow, or the weight of the pack causes me to stagger around my living room, suddenly aware of the way my vertebrae grind against each other. Then, I begin again, happily exposing my own frailties and foolishness. Do I really need a wire splint? Sticks and some duct tape would do. All this peanut butter! A Boy Scout couldn't eat that much in a month. Four pairs of socks—that's two pairs too many. I split the parachute line, throw out half the ibuprofen, abandon the raisins and most of the brown sugar. Then I feel guilty for wanting brown sugar at all.

Sometimes I stand in the kitchen and marvel at the array of pots, the stacks of company dishes and everyday dishes, the multiple spatulas, the piles of scorched pot holders, and I think, "A pot, a mug, and a spoon—that's all a person really needs." Surveying the pantry crowded with boxes and cans and bags, I recall Dunn's endorsement of the pioneer's fare: flour, beans, bacon, sugar, tea. If you want meat, then kill it.

The beautiful illusion of outfitting is in how carefully you must choose your gear. Not just any tent, not just any water bottle, but the *perfect* tent, bottle, pot, raincoat. I once spent many cheerful hours studying charts that compare backpacking cookstoves in terms of fuel efficiency, weight, optimum operating temperatures, reliability, cost. I ignored the stoves that resemble lunar landing modules, and the stoves that must be pumped, primed, and sweet-talked, and I chose the humblest device, because the worst time to fix a stove is when the wind is blowing sideways and the rain is falling cold and you've just dropped a crucial screw into the miniature jungle that is the tundra. But nothing has ever pleased me more than cooking with a driftwood fire on a lonely beach. Eliminating the stove altogether is the most elegant choice of all.

For a few hours after the fire, a bell jar surrounded my husband, me, and a loss whose size we could not yet calculate. And then, with the great whoosh of a vacuum unsealed, our best friends took us in, and more friends arrived, toting bulging garbage bags full of clothes, bedding, jewelry, belts, a stuffed cat, anything that could smother our pain. People offered us kittens, apartments, food. Just like that, we owned more than we could carry.

That first night, my husband and I slept in the skinny bed of our friends' five-year-old daughter. We stifled our crying so no one would hear us. That was the last time we cried together.

The next day I went to work wondering whose clothes I wore. Casserole sets, pots and pans, nightgowns—people could not stop donating. If they could not retrieve our old life for us, then they would erect a new one, with slightly different staging. My friend Martha gave me a delicate set of blue-and-white tea mugs, originally meant for a detested sister-in-law on her birthday. Fifteen years later, a single cup remains. At a "housewarming" party, we received cookbooks, artwork, a coffee grinder, all things I own still.

The day of the blaze, my husband returned alone to the house. Volunteer firefighters had found the dead cats tucked in hiding places in the ruined bedroom, and they shrouded them in a garbage bag and left them on the blackened porch. It was years before my husband told me how he had taken them to a trash bin and dropped them in, the irony being that in an ordinary death we would have had the animals cremated. I didn't ask for details then, and he didn't offer them. We couldn't bear each other's sadness and could not hand over the burden of our own.

Some backcountry travelers say you pack your insecurities. "Lots of weaknesses a man don't suspect he has, show up in this country," remarked one of Dunn's companions. The shed out back hides my own follies. A water-repellent sleeping bag cover purchased after several miserable nights in Glacier Bay but never used. A portable propane heater, which choked once and died. These things, and the many extra socks I pack obsessively, reveal that my weakness is an intolerance toward dampness, an odd quirk considering I grew up in a rain forest.

But it's not being wet I detest as much as what being wet signifies. Slouching around in soggy clothes or lying in a dank, dripping tent means now I'm vulnerable, not just to the weather but to my own faltering spirit. Spend one night truly wet and cold, and it's so easy to sink lower and lower, to fixate on all your troubles and worries, to imagine that you'll never be dry again, never warm up, never return home, where life was so damn easy all along and you just never noticed it.

Deeper fears can overwhelm you in this state, unreasonable fears. Capt. William Abercrombie, sent to build a military road from Valdez to Copper Center, described how the elements had affected prospectors who had spent the hellish winter of 1898–99 in the Copper River Valley. Many were destitute, frostbitten, and scurvy-ridden. "I noticed in talking to these people that over 70 per cent of them were more or less mentally deranged," he wrote. One man, a large Swede, explained that a glacial demon had strangled his son as they crossed the Valdez Glacier, despite the father's desperate struggle to tear the demon from his son's shoulders. The Swede brought his dead son down from the summit on a sled, and the other prospectors helped to bury the boy. Demons and bodies: two dreadful forms of impedimenta there.

You can't know until the time comes whether you're animated by that unnameable quality, that indefinable spark we call the survival instinct. That's my greatest fear, of course: that once the elements have overcome me, I won't be able to muster the fortitude necessary in difficult times. I'll break down, find myself mired in self-pity and lost to dread, become my own impedimenta.

There is a game I play sometimes, mentally rummaging through the pack, frisking my clothes, discarding gear, trying to discover the one thing I cannot do without.

The Leatherman is so shiny and clever, the way it collapses awls, blades, and files, the way it invents tools you didn't know you needed. But I could slice with a sharp stone, pierce with a stick, puncture with a splintered bone.

What about these stout matches and squat lighters that are waterproof, windproof, disposable, or indestructible? What about all the things I've set ablaze as firestarter? Dryer lint, birch bark, kerosene-soaked sawdust, potato chips. Better to study the diagrams of fire bows against the day when my pockets are empty.

I wouldn't keep the signaling devices, moleskin, extra socks, PowerBars. Not the sleeping bag: people lived a long time without Hollofil and Quallofil and five-denier continuous fiber insulation. Not the self-inflating pad: moss and branches will do. Not the water filter, the camp stove, the GPS. Not the fleece: furs are warmer, softer, more durable.

The bug dope? I confess to hesitating before tossing it aside.

The truth is, I won't know what I need most until I don't have it. But I would really hate to lose my boots. They are homely things: red-brown, tug-on, rubber XtraTufs, a brand known in these parts as Alaska tennis shoes. A friend convinced me they were sturdier and drier than Gore-Tex, Vibram, and other fabrications, and he was right. They don't breathe. They don't cushion. They just walk.

In them I have trod hillsides, waltzed across tussocks, forded rivers, plowed through muskeg, pushed through snow, dragged in sand. It's not clear whether my feet have shaped the boots or the boots have shaped my feet. After a hundred miles, a raggedy vent opened above the sole of the right boot, but the interior holds. That's how I hope to survive in life: battered but intact.

And so backpacking becomes a profession of faith in the self, a recollection, however fleeting, of all we once knew how to do: make fire, spear fish, knock birds from the sky, stalk game, skin carcasses, trap furbearers, evade predators, read weather, build shelter, birth in winter, bury dead in summer, twine knots, carry coals, construct canoes, bind wounds, locate water, protect our feet, cure bellyaches, pull teeth, splint bones, knap weapons, shape tools, weave grass into baskets and reeds into roofs, tame horses and dogs, find our way from here to there and back again, turn feelings into songs, make life into stories.

At the checkout counter of the grocery store, surrounded by the miraculous providence of Western society, I occasionally catch my hand creeping toward a magazine called *Real Simple*. Such a slick promise to make, when the very act of buying such a magazine negates the concept of simplicity.

Pot, mug, spoon, I remind myself sternly. Water, fire, shelter. Beans, bacon, tea.

And then I wonder if I couldn't live without the spoon and the cup, if the pot wouldn't be sufficient unto itself, if the beans can do without the bacon.

The notion of simplicity appeals because if you don't have much, what can you lose? A few days after the house burned down, we poked through the wreckage, and the greasy reek of soot was something we breathed inside ourselves. Remarkably, a few things had survived, but there was almost nothing I wanted anymore. I couldn't bear that stench.

One day, as we moved from one temporary apartment to another, my husband dropped a set of German crystal goblets, among the very few things that had mysteriously survived the flames. They shattered. He looked up at me, tensed for yet another thing to shatter between us. There was nothing to do but laugh.

All that was a long time ago. It was time, in fact, that eased our losses, time and the understanding that it was not our things that defined us, not even the loss of such things as books and cats and a certain innocent obliviousness, but rather our ability to press on together, no matter how much weighs upon us. Still, I wonder. I cannot leave a house without making sure the door is unlocked. My husband often returns to latch it behind me. There's a simple reason for my weakness. A neighbor had come to our burning house and tried to open the door, but it was locked. Probably the cats were already upstairs hiding beneath the bed.

Better to leave doors gaping, it seems to me. Better to let the world stroll in and take what it will of your fragile and temporary life.

I've learned to recognize a particular moment on a backcountry trip. It's the moment when I can't remember what I'm doing there. It usually comes after some grueling slog, after the pack mysteriously gains weight against all rules of fairness and physics. Everything rubs against me—the shoulder harness, the salt of my sweat, the relentless weather, the earth against my feet.

What is the point of this toil, this worry, this concentrated weight of all that must be carried?

It's like pushing through a membrane, that instant when misery transforms into surrender. Nothing becomes lighter, faster, easier. But now I can keep on, just for the power, the quiet ecstasy of keeping on, discarding burdens as I go, growing lighter and lighter with every step, because this—this freedom, this moment, this willingness to trust myself in an untrustworthy world—this is the one thing I cannot do without.

Turning Back

AT FIRST I THOUGHT OF THE HIKE along the old Circle-Fairbanks Trail as a walking meditation. For at least a week, maybe more, I would walk with only my blue heeler Jenny for company. I would spend all day, every day, quiet with my thoughts. For fifty-eight miles I would hike through heat and rain and mosquitoes on a hilly route I didn't know. On the other end, seven or eight days away, Scott, my husband, would greet someone different from the person he left at the trail-head. Of this I was sure.

For weeks I practiced with map and compass. I bought a GPS and learned to use it. I did girls push-ups twenty at a time. I filled my pack with the heaviest items—tent, sleeping bag, pad, clothes, stove, fuel, water filter—and marched along the first two miles of the trail to remind my feet and back of the task ahead. At the path's high points, I looked across the domes, patchy with snow, and imagined myself walking toward the horizon, soon.

I told all of my friends about the trip. It was a way of not chickening out. Some of them told me stories. One friend said, "I feel I should say that the worst mosquitoes I've ever encountered were on the Circle-Fairbanks Trail." Another described following the footprints of a solo hiker near the White River in the St. Elias Mountains until the footprints disappeared into the river, which is what happened to the hiker: he disappeared into the river after trying to float it in a small raft.

I could not help myself: I looked up news stories about him, and about other solo hikers, too. There was the thirty-six-year-old man who vanished in Glacier Bay National Park, leaving behind his tent, food, and most of his gear. The rangers decided he "strolled away from his camp, got lost, suffered hypothermia, and in his confusion fell into the water or crawled out of sight beneath a rock." What they meant was: "We have no idea what happened to him." There was the young woman who lost her way during a bird-watching day hike on one of the most popular trails near Fairbanks. Three days later, searchers found her but not her little dog, which had wandered off into the woods, to be eaten by bears or eagles or who knows what.

This was not the first time I would be alone out in the woods somewhere, but it was the first time I would hike such a distance by myself, relying on my own judgment, strength, skills. I would have to be brave. That's why I wanted to do it,

I suppose. At home I am the sort of person who is afraid to answer a ringing phone because a stranger might ask for something that I can't refuse, such as a donation to a suspiciously obscure charity or a subscription to a magazine I don't want. I spend long moments each day worrying about things that can't be changed, such as what I should have told the person on the phone instead of yes. I vex myself with imaginative dramas about things that haven't happened but could: falling elevators, mysterious diseases, wrongful criminal accusations. To a person who frets herself through daily life, it comes as a relief to lie awake nights and think through real problems: getting lost, falling ill, dying alone in some ravine.

Other, less definable worries occupied me, including how to keep a clear head no matter what. Never mind about losing the way—what about losing *it*, the all-important it that must be kept intact? Now and then I would stir restlessly and reach my hand toward my sleeping husband, trying to soothe that jumpy feeling in my chest. It was a familiar sensation, the fear of being afraid, of being so swamped by uncertainty and dread that I wouldn't know what to do. It was a feeling that had texture, dimension, weight.

The night before I left, I gathered the gear scattered about my living room and stuffed it into my big blue pack. When I hefted the load onto my back, I pitched backward a step, then forward, struggling to remain upright. Scott laughed. I took everything out and ditched whatever seemed excessive: extra bandages, a mini-disc recorder, rope. The pack lightened by perhaps nine or ten ounces. Surely this was the heaviest weight I had ever borne.

I did not know what else to leave behind. One person has to carry everything.

Scott drove me to the trailhead on a cool June morning. We climbed toward Cleary Summit on the Steese Highway, then turned onto bumpy dirt roads and ricketed toward the trailhead. Jenny paced back and forth across the backseat, smearing the windows with her muzzle. She was a dog who lived in constant anticipation. The radio repeated a news item about a thirty-year-old Alaskan killed the previous day when his truck rolled over. He had been a top athlete and a two-time competitor in the winter Wilderness Classic, an arduous 125-mile race through the Wrangell Mountains. Any day of the week, a person could die. A person doesn't have to slip down a mountainside, or get mauled by a bear, or disappear into the wilds to die. A person could drive to work and be killed, just like that.

Mosquitoes hummed in a thick fog at the trailhead. I grunted as I struggled into the pack and buckled myself to it. Scott attached a tinny bell to Jenny's collar. He sprayed me front and back with bug dope. He photographed us standing by the sign that said "Circle-Fairbanks Historical Trail," and the traitorous part of my brain wondered if that would be the picture they'd put in the paper once the search started. Scott had never once tried to dissuade me from this hike; he just assumed I knew what I was doing. He held my face and kissed me good-bye. "Be careful," he said, and I nodded mutely and turned up the trail. The next time I looked, he was driving away, and Jenny and I had no choice but to keep going.

The clouds evaporated as the day heated, and the mosquitoes dropped away in the sun. The pack's straps rasped against my collarbone. I leaned against a rocky slope and gulped water, letting it slop down my throat and chest. I offered Jenny a slurp and glanced at my watch. We had been walking for approximately thirteen minutes. Twenty minutes later, I trudged up a small slope to a rock outcropping, marked by beer cans and cigarette butts as a scenic overlook. Posts indicated each passing mile, but I hadn't seen the first marker yet. I was terribly afraid we hadn't reached it yet, because if it was going to take me an hour to walk a mile, then I might not get home before the end of summer.

A breeze stirred the creamy blooms of grass of Parnassus around our feet. "Thirsty?" I asked Jenny. She wagged her stub. A ridiculous tail for a dog. "Your tail is ridiculous," I told her. I could see I would be spending a lot of time talking to my dog. I missed Scott already. I heaved off the pack and poured water into Jenny's fold-up bowl. Then I sat on pointy rocks and drank deep drafts still cold from my kitchen faucet. Finding water would be a problem out here, but I could not stop gulping.

The hills roller-coastered around us. New leaves of aspens and birches riffled in the slow sea of air. A massive hard-rock gold mine named Fort Knox ground away in the distance, hidden from view. It was the newest quarry in a country that had been mined top to bottom for a hundred years. The maps are strewn with tiny Xs, hash marks, and crossed picks that symbolize prospects, mines, and tailings on every creek. Around here entire gold rush towns have long since eased back into the brush, leaving only names: Cleary, Gilmore, Golden City, Olnes. Pictures of Dome City, not far from the trailhead, show a thriving community built by former luminaries of the Klondike. The town included three banks, police and fire departments, a mayor, a stage company, and plenty of hotels and bars. Today—nothing.

The Circle-Fairbanks Trail is a narrow four-wheel drive road at the start, muddy and rutted with tracks from all-terrain vehicles, motorcycles, horses, moose, wolves, and bears. It is said the Athabascans originally used it, or some version of it, as a hunting and trade route. Then prospectors wandered through, frisking the creeks for gold. When diggings proved rich, lots of people suddenly had reason to travel from Circle City on the Yukon River into the Birch Creek region. When a scruffy Italian prospector named Felix Pedro panned colors from a creek not far from this dome, hopeful people poured in from the Yukon and the Chandalar country to a new gold camp named Fairbanks.

Mail, cattle, sheep, passengers, and supplies crossed the country between Circle City and Fairbanks. So much gold traversed this route that the "Blue Parka Bandit" shadowed the trail, politely but firmly robbing stages and lone miners of their fortunes. In 1928, the Steese Highway borrowed some of the trail, and then there wasn't much reason to use the rest. Most of the roadhouses closed, and the route lapsed, used only by dog mushers, snowmachiners, hikers, horse riders, and off-road riders. A few stubborn miners drive the trail to their claims, but the rest of us use it for fun.

I rolled my pack over and loosened the shoulder cinches. In a process that seemed to grow harder each time rather than easier, I hoisted it to one bent knee, wormed my right arm through the strap, twisted my left arm behind my back, and, stooping over, tugged it onto my back. Involuntary sounds emerged from my mouth that I thought I wouldn't be making for another twenty or thirty years. "Mother of God, why is this pack so heavy?" I groaned. Jenny stared at me, ears perked, pink tongue dangling wetly. "Why aren't you wearing a pack?" I asked. "You could at least carry your own food."

Recently I'd begun to wonder if her sharp eyes—eyes that could spot a bread crumb falling onto the floor from ten feet away—had clouded a little. Sometimes I had to clap my hands to catch her attention. Her muzzle had whitened, and she no longer made wild, acrobatic leaps to catch Frisbees. In dog years she was ninety-one. Bringing her along seemed a bit like dragging your grandmother on the Appalachian Trail. Nevertheless, I assumed Jenny would like walking with me, and of course, at first she did. What a grand creature a dog is.

Until now, I hadn't given much thought to the actual hiking. Mostly I'd concentrated on simply getting here. Several weeks earlier I had spent three days in the hospital when outpatient surgery had unexpectedly become inpatient surgery. For a time, the diagnosis had been vague, and alarming words had been bandied about—"growth" and "malignant" and so on. I'd signed papers authorizing the removal of any suspicious tissue, up to and including entire reproductive organs—not that the doctor expected such a thing, he kept saying. During the procedure, the surgeons discovered I was suffering from endometriosis, a fairly common problem in which uterine tissue colonizes new territory, but they had been forced to abandon the minor procedure of a laparoscopy, with its modest nick through the belly button, and instead had slit open my lower abdomen and mucked about in my internal organs, leaving me with a six-inch scar and a sore belly.

I had shared the hospital room with an eighty-year-old woman who'd had removed an abdominal tumor the size of a basketball, a tumor she hadn't known was there until she'd undergone a scan for back problems. She was proud of a Polaroid documenting her remarkable tumor, a photograph I repeatedly fended off. My doctor, though, ambushed me in the follow-up exam with Technicolor pictures of my body cavity with organs splayed out during surgery. I wasn't sure which was worse: actually seeing my own innards, or knowing that total strangers had been photographing them while I was as insensible as I ever hope to be this side of death.

I spent a good part of the spring huffing at crunches, scratching the red scar that embossed my belly, trying to regain a feeling of wholeness and strength. This hike would prove my health, my vigor, my endurance. Still I couldn't seem to shake the red truth of that photograph.

I sang. It seemed early in the trip to holler spirit-bolstering songs, but I sang anyway. I stepped among the tracks of all who had passed recently—horses, people, wolves, a moose and her newborn calf—and I sang lullabies and hymns, love songs, and ditties composed entirely of nonsense. Jenny paced and panted just behind me. Usually she insisted on leading any expedition. When she was younger, it drove her to distraction on berry-picking expeditions if any of us wandered about; she spent all her energy trying to herd us into one safe, compact group. Today the heat seemed to have dulled her usual energy, and she lagged. Whenever we paused, she flopped in the dirt and waited, eyes half-closed.

Jenny didn't like me when we first got her as a repo dog, thirteen years before. Scott's boss had bred heelers, also known as Australian cattle dogs, and he had retrieved Jenny from her new owners when he discovered that the puppy was living night and day in a garage lined with Visqueen on the floor. He next sold her to a man who never asked his wife if she wanted a dog. She didn't. A week later, I was visiting Scott at work when the embarrassed man returned with a gray-and-red puppy that rocketed around at near the speed of light, ears flattened, tongue curled. We took her home.

She was four months old and had missed crucial time being socialized. She bared her teeth and rolled her eyes suspiciously whenever I tried to pet her, no matter how much I complimented her fine markings, the black that circled her eyes like kohl and tipped her ears, the silvery sheen of her coat and her ruddy belly, the white streak on her fawn-colored face. Within a few days, she decided to be my dog after all, a job she took far too seriously. It was years before she would let anyone else in the house without terrifying them, though once she did warn me about a man I was too stupid to realize was dangerous. Most of her attitude problems I attributed to chronic underemployment. Lacking cows to organize, she bossed around our two cats and the other dog, a male husky-Lab who was much larger than she was but who had the intelligence of a sharp-witted pet turtle. Jenny had not only brains but also opinions she couldn't keep to herself. We called her piercing yap the "Vulcan Death Bark."

Unfortunately, she did not see me as the alpha female so much as an outsize littermate who occasionally made irritating demands and was not particularly accommodating about sharing the bed. But everywhere I went, she followed, even from room to room in the house. "Mind your own beeswax," I chided her one day, and Scott said, "But you are her beeswax." Out here, it was comforting being somebody's beeswax.

At every milepost I stopped and entered the position in my GPS. It tracked my progress, but the satellite readings told me nothing my feet and back didn't know already. Mile two, uphill on a wooded slope. Mile three, along a forested straightaway, passing a leghold trap on the trail. Mile four, curving upward against the outside of a dome, where a runnel of clear water dribbled from the thawing tundra. Mile five, alongside two fresh sets of bear tracks pressed into the mud.

We passed an explosion of white-gray fur, and I panicked briefly when I saw Jenny nosing a caribou leg near the trail. For all I knew, that pair of bears lurked nearby protecting a kill. A prickly, urgent feeling quickened my steps. "Let them in, Peter. They are very tired," I bellowed tunelessly. "Give them couches where the angels sleep, and light those fires." But I didn't like the trend of that song, rooted as it was in the afterlife, so I switched to love songs. It's my belief that bears like love songs best.

The mucky trail turned toward the summit, and so had the bears. I labored on, sweat tracking my face as we rose above the tree line. Just below the dome's crown, I dropped my pack with an oof. For lunch I tired my jaws on jerky as I studied the ranks of black, dense clouds drifting in from the east and searched the tundra for dark shapes nosing through the vegetation. Jenny waited at my feet for the wads of jerky I couldn't conquer. Bear sign didn't alarm her. The possibility that I might not share lunch did.

On the downhill, my left foot slipped, and I toppled over in slow motion, gravity pulling the pack onto me. Jenny sniffed at my face pressed against cool mud. I laughed, but this would not do. On my top five list of things I did not want to go wrong: sprains, breaks, or twists of any sort. Pay attention, I scolded myself. Every moment demands attention.

This wasn't all about overcoming fear. I didn't know how else to see the world more clearly than to walk through it. I could not think of a better way to be quiet for a while. True, now that I was here, for long minutes I did not look any higher than my own feet, step by deliberate step up and down those long hills. It was also true that I felt compelled to announce our approach to the wild animals of the country in song and chant, and to speak often to my dog, and to offer a few encouraging words to myself.

But there were these moments, too, when I stopped for no reason that could be named, and stood silently in the middle

of the trail, head back, one more person on the way to somewhere that can't be mapped.

A gnarl of thunder followed flashbulb pulses of lightning. Fog
and darkness cloaked the distant hills—the hills we headed
toward. The only thing I know about lightning is that there's
nothing good about being the tallest object on a treeless dome.
I walked faster until an upward thrust of shale appeared and
offered shelter for the tent. Rain pecked against the fly, and
Jenny snorted as she slept, ears twitching whenever thunder
ripped close by. The nylon flapped in the wind, but the struc-
ture held. A few inconstant drips rolled into the dog's water
dish, the pot, and the water bottle. All this rain and we'd
harvest but a mouthful. I pulled on long johns and rain gear,
leaned against the pack, and dozed.

At 5 p.m., as the storm drifted southward, I screwed
the stove together outside the tent while I crouched inside.
Flames shot toward my face as I twisted the fuel nozzle the
wrong way. Fire lapped at the tent door before I could turn
the stove off. My face still warm, I moved the entire setup
to a nearby rock and tried again. The pot had just started
bubbling when it slipped, spilling stroganoff fixings across
the rocks. "This is why we won't sleep where we eat," I told
Jenny, who began industriously licking up lumpy sauce and
crunchy noodles. So far, a few hours into our trip, I had nar-
rowly avoided twisting my ankle, searing my face, and setting
our shelter on fire.

The trail lurched downhill through a boggy black spruce forest until it crossed a dirt track headed toward the Kokomo Creek mine. Jenny waded into a muddy yellow pond to drink and cool off. I dug out a water bag; as dirty as it was, the scummy pond represented the most water we'd seen in four miles.

An empty five-gallon bucket lay beside the trail, and I wondered about bear-baiting stations. Most any bear would run from us with enough warning, but a bear accustomed to slumming around mine camps, digging freebies out of trash cans, and being deliberately attracted by rotting food was exactly the kind of bold bear I feared the most. My thoughts ping-ponged now between sore feet and the bear tracks we'd crossed. All I carried was the pepper spray, a small flare for scare value, and an arsenal of Carpenters' songs, which I now grunted, one word per step.

We passed a sign lying in a ditch: "CAUTION. This and all trails are being trapped. Traps and snares in and along trails. Use with caution." The words "Trap Theives" were lettered within a circle and slash mark. The misspelling made it seem more ominous. Marten sets appeared periodically along the trail, with diagonal poles nailed to a tree, and some shiny trinket—a few inches of tinsel garland, can lids, or even CDs—hanging above the set to mark it.

I revisited my list of top five worries. Perhaps more than injuring myself, I feared that Jenny would get hurt by wandering into an abandoned trap or snare. I carried a small first-aid kit jammed with a wire splint; cold pack; gauze and Band-Aids; antibiotic ointments and antiseptic wipes; pills for diarrhea, urinary tract infections, runny noses, and miscellaneous aches and pains. But I was not sure I could do anything for an injured dog.

At mile nine, I stopped to set up the tent in a gravelly clearing, proud to have exceeded my daily goal by a mile. Jenny snoozed on moss among the trees as I struggled with the tent, which was actually a tarp with a mesh insert for sleeping. Hiking sticks acted as the poles.

I filtered muddy water and filled her dish and my bottle, dosing mine with lemonade crystals to help me choke it down. She licked the dinner pot of leftover rice and beans. She was a terrible chowhound. We had stopped storing cat food cans on the pantry floor when Jenny began shredding them open with her teeth.

I dragged the pack into the bushes but took the pepper spray and signal flare into the tarp. It was hot in there, the black mesh amplifying the sun's rays. A violent hum of mosquitoes and buzz-sawing of wasps enveloped the mesh like a force field. The night would never grow dark, only dim, and for this I was glad. Now and then my mind circled around the game trails emerging from the trees, picturing moose bursting out and trampling the tarp, or a bear moseying into the open, sniffing after my pack, but there was no profit in those thoughts. Every couple of hours I stirred long enough to peer outside. Close to dawn, the quiet was liquid, something you'd have to push against to move through. Even the mosquitoes had disappeared. A fine dew misted the tarp and the sleeping bag.

At 8 a.m., the dog and I yawned in each other's faces and then stiffly sat up and stretched. There is a certain kind of earned pain that feels good, that reminds you that your body can almost always do more than you think it can. She looked at the kibble I poured into the pot lid and then looked at me. I sighed and spooned some of my oatmeal with brown sugar and raisins onto her food. Then she ate.

At 10 a.m., we took our first tender steps on the trail. Blue sky. No clouds. Not enough water. Already I was hot. And thirsty. I was very thirsty.

Ahead the trail climbed and dropped over the two- and three-thousand-foot hills. Today we'd be hiking hard if we wanted to cover eight miles. I occupied myself thinking up new songs, taking that old chestnut "Bingo" and improvising verses to flatter my dog: "There was a doggy I called my own, and Jenny was her name-o. J-E-N-N-Y, J-E-N-N-Y . . . " I hoped no one would hear. It's the kind of thing saps do with their dogs, like giving them nicknames for any occasion: Jennifer Dogifer, Flufferbutt, Pigger Dog, Doodlebrain, Miss Bossy. Her ears radared my way as she wondered why I kept calling her when she was standing right there.

As the trail started rising even more steeply, I switched to army chants: "We are climbing up this hill. We will make it, yes we will. Won't be the first, won't be the last. We are going to kick its ass. Sound off, one, two, sound off, three, four . . ." I was my own sergeant and recruit, song leader and chorus. Basically, I was doing all the work.

In some ways, traveling with no one but a dog for companionship was ideal. I could stop whenever I wanted. The dinner menu required no polite consultations. Nobody would drop helpful little hints about better ways to erect the tent or build fires. I could pee wherever I wanted. Acting cheerful when I didn't feel cheerful was not required. But a partner who could talk had advantages. It would be nice to say out loud, "Man, this hill is a bitch," and have someone pause and wipe his or her forehead and say, "You can say that again."

By noon, only a few mouthfuls of tea-colored water remained in the bottle. I stopped at every trickle, pumped brown sludge from pools gathered in moose tracks as Jenny slurped away. I couldn't afford to be picky; no streams bubbled merrily along the route, no crystalline ponds waited, no rivers rushed by. There were only potholes and a few patches of stale snow in the shadows.

I had already used my compass to correctly divine the proper direction at a confusing fork. Now wayfinding depended on the trail itself and a vague, faint pencil sketch that I had transferred from a trail brochure to my map. At the next fork, I studied the rougher uphill path to the left. The thick dashes marking the trail on the wrinkled brochure were dismayingly ambiguous. They could signify either route—over the dome, or just below it. I turned right to continue on the well-used route we had followed successfully so far. It dipped down and seemed to round the dome just below the summit rather than crossing over the top.

A fire had swept over these slopes several years back, leaving blackened aspen trunks twisting out of the greenery. I kept on, unease growing as I failed to pass milepost 14 or

15. We stopped for lunch and more water filtering as I studied the map and worried. When the trail dropped downhill abruptly, I stopped and pulled out the GPS, compass, and maps again. "You're not lost if you know where you are," I told myself fiercely. I sighted on the hill below. The trail should head northeast. This route was now clearly trending southeast.

A little while before, I thought I might cry if I discovered we had taken the wrong route. But now I did not feel like crying. I felt tired and mad at myself. Why didn't I pause at that fork to think things through? Why had I been so sure? This was when having a human partner would be good—someone to argue with, to help you rassle with problems, to blame. But now I had done something stupid and there was nothing for it but to retrace our steps two miles backward and uphill. There was no one to scold me, either, so I called myself a dumbshit just to make myself feel better.

My legs ached as the hill steepened. It was almost 4 p.m., and now our mileage lagged behind schedule. After a mile we plodded past a rough, mysterious track that jolted upward. I paused to consider. As steep as the path was, I felt certain it headed to the ridgetop and intersected the Circle-Fairbanks Trail in a shortcut. I braced my trekking poles in the mud and pushed.

Every few steps, we stopped so I could suck air. The route was not perfectly vertical; it only seemed that way. I mumbled songs to create a rhythm. Hike for a verse, stop. Hike for a verse, stop. Water trickled through ruts. The alders thinned, but I blew my whistle now and then in case bears idled unseen. The sky blackened above the ridge as the daily thunderstorm approached. A solid wind pushed against us as we took the last, struggling steps onto the ridge, where low alpine flowers shuddered. Ahead, the saddle dropped sharply into a spruce-draped valley. Greening hills, hummocky and mottled from cloud shadows, rolled out before us, and the Crazy Mountains surfed in peaks. To the left, a bald dome. To the right, an even steeper hill. I strained to see if the lump on top was a cairn, or trail marker. I couldn't tell for sure. Now I regretted leaving binoculars behind just to save a few ounces.

I dragged the pack behind a rocky bluff and pitched the tarp against the coming rain. My feet ached, and the skin joining my big toes to the footpad was raw. Jenny flopped in the lichens and watched me with her head on her paws.

Inside the tent, I fell into the pleasurable daze that comes when your feet don't have to move. Every time the wind lifted the tarp's nylon edges, I studied the dome behind us in brief glimpses, searching for a trail. Perhaps there was no obvious route because people could cross the dome's bare flanks any way they pleased. I imagined faint trails through the lichens and low brush. Tomorrow we'd leave early to make up for wasted miles.

When the wind failed, the mosquitoes rose up, a hidden wave of attackers that had discovered the only warm-blooded creatures for miles. I decided to shift the tarp to face the sun, and rather than walking around to tug out the stakes, I yanked at the taut ropes. A heavy plastic stake snapped from the ground and smacked against my face before I could react. My lip went numb, and blood oozed down my chin. In the compass mirror I studied the welt splitting my lower lip.

Dear Diary: I am one grand adventurer. On Day One I almost set my eyebrows and the tent on fire. On Day Two I took the wrong trail and then belted myself in the face and dripped blood all over the tundra. On Day Three, a bear tracked the scent and ate me up.

In the tent, Jenny curled at my feet, but every few minutes she sat up and licked at her right hind flank. "Mosquito bites? Poor doggy," I said. My commiseration meant nothing to her. Tomorrow I'd rub a little bug dope over her fur. Tomorrow I'd be much more careful about fire and maps. Tomorrow we'd be in the alpine, high above the world, and well on our way to serenity.

Through the night, Jenny's licking became so frantic and compulsive that I woke several times as she shook the tent, jarring loose hundreds of mosquitoes attached to the mesh, intoxicated by the carbon dioxide. I surveyed the tundra each time I woke. A cotton-candy sky rimmed the horizon, and dawn's sparrows lilted in the brush. Low twists of willow and dwarf birch and berry bushes glowed with a faint green haze as spring settled in the alpine.

In the morning, when I sat up, cramped and sore, Jenny was still lapping at her hindquarters. Animals in pain have a glazed, unfocused look; I recognized it in her. She had licked her leg until the fur was sopping, and drool puddled on the tent floor and soaked the sleeping bag. I groaned aloud. "What? What is it?" I asked. Clearly something was wrong, but all she did was eye me and then return to nibbling and licking. She showed me her teeth when I reached toward her leg.

Jenny didn't seem to limp, but she dropped into the soft tundra after we climbed out of the tent and occasionally nosed at her trembling flank. Bugs settled on her muzzle and her eyes. In the old days, backcountry travelers simply shot crippled animals and moved on. If she lamed up, I could not possibly carry her to the trail's end, nor could I leave her. I looked out across the hills where green lay upon green, to the southern horizon and the white illuminati of the Alaska Range.

The reasons for making this trip now rose clear and hard before me. One was pride, the ego boost of being able to mention casually that once I had hiked by myself for a week, just me and my dog, through the backcountry. I had announced this trip widely. How could I return now having walked only fifteen miles?

Part of it, I admitted, was the hope of encountering some kind of inner peace, maybe even an epiphany, which was the very thing I criticized others for seeking in the wilderness. Probably that was because I desired it so much myself. The last time I had spent a week alone in the woods, fear and loneliness had dropped me to my knees, and then a calmness had fallen upon me, as cool and needful as the wind moving through the crowns of ancient trees.

Out here, by myself, I could be honest: Hadn't I made this journey as a way of finding that peace again? After this spring's frightening surgery, didn't I count on some kind of spiritual transformation as a reward for walking a week by myself, for facing my fears? Wasn't I expecting to be struck like a gong sometime along this trail, to vibrate with all the meaning and intensity possible when one climbs a lesser mountain, under a pale sun at midnight, alone? And I had learned nothing so far except all the foolish things of which I was capable.

But now I did know about something else: the pain of turning back. This was the mildest of journeys, and yet for the first time I understood a little why explorers sometimes made such excellent liars. Frederick Cook stood on a minor ridge of Mount McKinley and took the photographs that he hoped would fool the world. He had to; how could he again fail in his quest to summit? Few things are sadder and less interesting than someone who turns back before reaching the top, the pole, the end of the world, or the end of the trail.

Companion and journalist Robert Dunn mocked Cook's pretensions during their first unsuccessful attempt on Mount McKinley. But as they crept up the most dangerous slopes, unroped and weak with hunger, he found himself admiring the doctor's steadiness and cursing his own fear. "As for me, is the doing of a thing to be no longer its end, as was in the old adventurous days?" he asked. "The telling of it the end instead?" And here I was, on my little jaunt over well-trod ground, with neither a doing nor a telling to show for it.

How much easier to be a prospector than an adventurer. Looking for gold was a solid reason to roam around these hills. But looking for glory, or looking for God—that's just asking for failure.

Jenny watched as I melted snow by the potful. This is your decision now, I thought. Just make it and don't second-guess yourself. Just live with it.

I cried. This is something wilderness is good for: crying as loudly as you want, letting tears and snot run down your face as you shake and sob. I cried because this was not the summer I would walk alone after all. I cried because I hate retracing my steps. I cried because the shadowed hills ahead would not reveal their mysteries to me.

And I cried because every time I looked at my old dog's face I could see death in it. I knew she would die some day, of course. We all will. You know it and I know it, but we know it as dispassionately as a memo, as formally as a warranty that we glance at once and then tuck away in a junk drawer. There is no gut truth in such knowledge. But in that moment I knew that my dog would die before long, and soon enough, I will, too. I myself had seen the red and slick tenderness of my own organs. I had seen the future in a lonely old woman holding out a Polaroid of a tumor the size of a basketball.

This was my only discovery: that I had reached the place where middle age tips into loss, when everything worth caring about begins to disappear—not just my beloved dog, but relatives, friends, my husband, time itself and all its possibilities. For two days I had walked just to arrive at this place, just so I could recognize that in life there is no turning back.

I looked at my dog, lying quietly in the tundra, dark eyes fixed upon me, ears flicking away mosquitoes. There was no dishonor in attending to her. I thought of all the accounts I'd read of people and dogs in the north. For every act of indifference or cruelty, there was some old miner or explorer who valued his dog above any person, any gold. Only history remembers the husky named Mose, owned by a Klondiker who told an admirer: "Mister, don't ask me to place a value on my partner. I couldn't think of it! Why, if I should lose my poke of dust, rather than to part with Mose, we would hit the trail back and try for another raise."

I could always take this trail again, add my steps to the long procession of Athabascans, stampeders, freighters, bandits, thru-travelers, all of us collaborating on keeping this passage open across the landscape. So few people anymore know the country this way, step by step, hill by hill. Someday I would return. Just not with my dog, who was moving faster than I toward what awaits us all.

I drank deeply of melted snow from the winter past and washed myself clean with what remained. I collapsed the tarp and shook out my sleeping bag and arranged my pack carefully, for we had a long way to travel. I sat on a rock and inspected my feet and babied my blisters and pulled my boots back on. I climbed the bluff to sit and memorize the hazy wash of green in the valleys and the silver gleam of unknown mountains. With every step I crushed perfect alpine flowers flecking the tundra like confetti.

Jenny followed me, as is her way. For this little while, we were high above the world, pausing on a path each one of us travels through life.

Then, finally, I tied the bell back onto her collar so I could always find her and I hoisted the pack to my shoulders. It had not lightened a bit. I looked northward once, thinking, *It's not too late to keep on. You've been wrong so many times already. You could take a chance that she'll be all right.*

But even as I turned back, I could feel the sorrow and beauty of the world sinking through me, settling into my flesh, as firm and necessary as the bones that would have to carry me along this trail.

Circumnavigation

WE WERE SITTING IN THE BREAKWATER BAR, the sailors and I, planning the upcoming race around Admiralty Island. We had drilled ourselves hard during sprint races up and down Gastineau Channel, shaking down *Lyric* and ourselves. We had jibed and tacked, raised sails and lowered them, flung ourselves from port to starboard.

I was not a sailor. I was a reporter, an observer, an initiate. I was cargo, along for the ride. The sailors promised to teach me something about sailing, and I promised not to fall overboard. My mind still fumbled with the purer science of sailing, with the idea that sails sculpt wind to draw power. Every time the sailors spoke of aerodynamic force, hull resistance, drag ratios, and thrust, I nodded, but I heard only math, not magic.

Now my arms ached as if I had been hoisting bags of cement. Broken blisters oozed on my palms. I washed the taste of brine from my lips with ale, recalling the way *Lyric* coursed around the stodgy tugboats, nipped under the towering bow of an anchored ocean liner.

For the article, and for myself, I asked the sailors casually, "Why race around Admiralty Island?" It is something they do every summer solstice, launching themselves on a 210-mile circumnavigation around the huge island and back to Juneau. They sail night and day, pausing only for an overnight stop at Baranof Warm Springs. For a week they run away to sea, deserting families, jobs, identities. They call the race "The Spirit of Adventure," and it's true it offers most elements of the best Alaskan contests: potential disaster, a test of skills undervalued by society, the chance to be pummeled by awful weather, a certain grandeur of vision, and relative pointlessness. It is practically irresistible.

The sailors considered my question, and then, in the intimate manner of the mildly intoxicated, one of them leaned against me and said the race illustrates the three essential conflicts she learned about in high school literature. She ticked them off against her fingers: Man against man. Man against nature. Man against self.

"Bullshit," said her fellow sailor, the one drinking Jack Daniel's. "It's all about terror and ecstasy." That seemed right. We all raised our glasses to terror and ecstasy.

On the morning of the race, I lugged my waterproof duffel down the causeway of Harris Harbor. Swaddled in fog and drizzle, the world dissolved around the edges. The town of Juneau glistened and pulsed like a mirage, houses and buildings fading in and out. Douglas Island appeared to be drifting away from the mainland. Nothing resembled the certain lines of charts and maps I had studied the night before, hoping to memorize the outlines of the place we were sailing into.

From childhood on, I had explored local waters in all manner of vessels—as large and utilitarian as the state ferries, as small as my thirteen-foot skiff. On the water, I always moved slowly and gently, as if in the company of a wild animal whose attention I don't wish to attract. They were the best days, those spent fishing for salmon coursing at unknown depths, or searching for whales near Shelter Island, or visiting uninhabited islands no larger than a high school gymnasium. Marine charts flag known dangers—lurking reefs, the thrust of rocks, unexpected shoals. But what I worried about was not marked on any chart I had ever seen. No navigational symbols warned of the absolute and utter way the sea can claim you, the complete indifference of its force. Even in the finest weather, I never forgot how quickly it can change—how fast wind can rise, how steadily waves can beat themselves higher and higher until, suddenly, returning to shore becomes not a matter of will but of absolute attention. And luck. Luck never hurts.

I descended the slippery gangway carefully, holding back against the steep cant. The tide was out. Boats of all character nudged the creaking docks like restless horses in a stable. Ravens hunched in the mist, one to a piling. In this unpromising dawn, I felt reluctant to abandon land's sweet and certain hold, so it was a relief to glance up and see three great blue herons floating overhead, their wings as silent and ashen as the clouds. A good omen, I thought. Forget the charts. Cling to portents.

Lyric rocked and swayed as the sailors stowed gear and unsnapped sail covers. A twenty-seven-foot Catalina, she was shaped like the camber of a gull's wing. But framed by the slip, she seemed cramped and slight among the comfortable houseboats, the sturdy fishing boats that smelled of sea and offal, the gleaming pleasure vessels. *Lyric*'s spars looked reedy and bare without sails. The five of us stepped carefully around each other; the cabin was smaller than a college dorm room, the cockpit smaller yet. Except for the married couple who owned the boat, none of us knew each other well. I wondered if we would be speaking to each other at race's end.

The sailors checked lines and hoisted sails as we motored out of the harbor and into Gastineau Channel. A stiff breeze snapped the white cloth until we trimmed the sails tight as drumheads by hauling on the sheet ropes. The boat vibrated, strummed by wind and motion. With fourteen other sailboats, most larger than *Lyric*, we circled the bobbing markers like sharks, waiting for the 8 a.m. start flag. The sailors shouted insults at other boats cutting across our bow as skippers maneuvered for a good opening. My nervousness evaporated in the high spirits.

When the red flag shot up the start boat's mast, we surged into a commotion of sails and bows and cheers. At the mark, *Lyric* tacked sharply across the channel, but boats in better positions outpointed us, sailing closer to the wind and quickly gaining distance. Our enthusiasm ebbed as we fell behind. We were not the last boat, but we were not far ahead of it. A lot can happen on this race, the sailors told each other. Just wait. We'll catch up.

We split into two shifts, and the other watch went below, beginning our schedule of three hours on, three hours off. A steady headwind lulled us into a rhythm of tacking back and forth across the channel, but the tide flowed against us, and we didn't actually seem to be going anywhere. Mesmerized by the scrolling waves, I lapsed into a cottony reverie. A fair-weather boater only, I have always tethered myself close to shore, allowing only my imagination to hover over the abyss. Long ago this coast was named and charted, but I yearned to feel what the early explorers did as they slipped into bays, rounded dark islands, searched the unfamiliar sky and water for omens. Everything they encountered became a revelation. Seldom in our lives do we have the chance to set sail toward a new world.

Not everyone returns, even from the most modest of expeditions. Boats are found drifting, or never found at all. Wreckage washes up on empty shores. Bodies float low like waterlogged driftwood, nibbled into anonymity by the sea and its creatures. From the safety of land we invent fates for those who don't come back. Sea lions capsized their kayaks. He hit his head and fell overboard. A rogue wave crashed over the stern. Lost at sea, we say, they are lost at sea. Once I read about a lighthouse keeper who took a small boat to cut a Christmas tree near Cross Sound. But the engine died, and the ocean carried him away. His partner last saw him sitting in the skiff with arms akimbo, as calm as if he had already accepted the great blankness that awaited him. Fishermen who searched for him finally found the empty boat a hundred miles away.

A thump against the hull startled us. I turned to gauge how far we had sailed in the past few hours, but grayness had closed behind us. Ahead, Gastineau Channel opened into a great bowl of sea rimmed by shadowy islands. We looked about for whatever knocked against the boat—driftwood? a loose buoy?—until the best sailor emerged from the cabin, recognized the sloppy way the mainsail spilled air, and shouted at us. Under bracing gusts of curses, we tightened the sails and ourselves. He seized the tiller, and the boat quickened under his sure hand.

Just as we broke the tide's grip and slipped into Stephens Passage, a southeasterly wind gulped us whole. Before, it had all seemed so familiar: the same endless trinity of ocean, mountain, and forest. Suddenly, I recognized nothing. Whitecaps curled as four-foot seas climbed up each other. Spray whipped off waves the way blowing snow streams from mountain peaks. Like a bully in a schoolyard fight, thirty-five-knot winds shoved *Lyric* over, testing how far she would heel without capsizing. Hard rain stuttered across the water. The boat surged and tossed, and waves spewed over the bow.

My stomach churned, from motion sickness and perhaps panic. I had never taken the wind so personally. Somehow I felt that my fear invoked this storm. I should have known better than to venture into waters I didn't know, with people who were strangers, on a boat I didn't really understand. All I could do was crouch in the stern and stare at the mainland, trying to fix my eyes on something stable.

Time lost hold of us as *Lyric* beat on long tacks that drew us close to Admiralty Island's rocky, log-strewn shores, then swept us away. We swung on the end of a pendulum, motion without progress. The sails bellied and strained with too much wind, overpowering the boat. Eventually, the sailors climbed into neon-orange survival suits and strapped on lifelines. Two of them staggered onto the foredeck to reef the mainsail, diminishing its size to reduce the wind's effect. For the first time, I realized there was no spare survival suit for me. I cast about, thinking of things that float. Ice chest? Seat cushions in the cabin? I tried to remember if anyone had shown me where the life jackets were stowed.

I stopped worrying about flotation devices when I realized the port-side rails lining the deck were dashing over and over into the foaming black water. Instinctively, I leaned away from that side of the boat. In our practice runs, the captain assured me that he had never dipped the side rails. I thought hard about this, trying to understand exactly what he meant. Surely he hadn't lied. But could this actually have been the first time the boat had heeled over that far? Did that mean this was the worst storm he had ever sailed in? Did he really know what he was doing? Watching the rails submerge repeatedly, I tried to sense through the hull that fulcrum beyond which the boat would not roll upright again.

The sailors returned to the mast and braced themselves against the heaving foredeck. They ducked their heads against the rain as they dropped the mainsail in jerks and prepared to raise a smaller one. The wind shrouded them in canvas, and they struggled against the wet sail while trying to keep their footing. When they shoved the mainsail toward us to stuff into the cabin, I studied their faces for signs of fear, or worse, but I saw only ferocious concentration and a kind of crazed exhilaration.

As the gale continued and the sailors tired, they decided to conserve strength by returning to our watch schedule. I gathered my helplessness and went below. The others dug themselves into sleeping bags and instantly dozed. I slumped on a berth and stared through the opposite porthole, captured by the way the pitching window presented alternating views of clouds before it plunged below the green-black water. Sky, then sea. Sky, then sea.

The cabin was close and humid, and my dread escaped the mental chokehold I had clamped upon it. I imagined being trapped below deck should the boat capsize. Then I saw myself in my yellow slicker, struggling toward dim green light above. Frigid water poured into my boots and flooded my overalls, dragging me below. I swallowed the sea. It filled my mouth and lungs and belly. Down and down I drifted, hands limp and white, hair floating upward. My eyes remained open in the darkness, the cold ocean pressing against them.

And then I dwelled on my private horror: crabs settling on my body, flounders writhing across me, colonies of small creatures slipping under my clothes and then under my skin, picking and chewing and gnawing.

I mourned my husband, as if he were lost to me, and not I to him.

The intense desire to throw up shoved panic away. I felt almost grateful. Surely I couldn't be so far gone if I feared the humiliation of puking in the cabin more than drowning in it. Climbing topside, I reeled to the stern and vomited in wrenching bursts. The sailors didn't notice. I was glad; it's one thing to die, but another to die as a known coward. I leaned against the gunwale, head hanging overboard, and watched the way waves folded into each other, green marble skeined by white foam. Cold rain soaked my head and sopped my jacket collar. Even the insides of my ears were wet. I was too miserable to pray, so over and over I pictured the morning's three herons and the solemn way they winged out of the fog.

I didn't know when I realized the gale was subsiding, the sound of high weather fading like a distant radio station. I would have been relieved if I were not so tired, so bruised by fear. This is only the first day, I thought; what else could happen during our journey? I longed to be home, back in my ordinary life.

At 9 p.m., the watch changed, and it was time to be useful. My shift tried to regain lost time by harvesting failing winds to power *Lyric* across the strait. How peaceful, this serene motion across a calming sea. Our tasks seemed so simple after the afternoon's frantic efforts.

One sail floated behind us, a white signal against the dimming light. For all our impotent motion, we were still not last. The other ships forged ahead along the storm's edge. Later, when we heard that *Arrogant*'s mainsail blew out and *Casa Mia*'s seacocks flooded with water, I felt absurdly satisfied knowing that my fear wasn't misplaced.

Across the passage, darkness flowed from sea into sky. When it was time to go below, I wedged myself into a bunk, still wearing wet clothes that twisted and rubbed uncomfortably against the damp sleeping bag. Sleep was a wave rolling me over and over against the shore. When the sailor who wanted my bunk shook me awake for the 3 a.m. to 6 a.m. shift, I mumbled, "Okay," but the absence of motion confused me. For several dazed moments, I didn't know where I was.

On deck, cool air washed against my face. Indistinct shapes crowded the horizon. Far off—impossible to say how far, in this flat light—icebergs as big as houses glowed with their own faint blue auras. I propped myself against the gunwales and drowsed, tucking my hands under my arms for warmth. My head dangled painfully, lolling against my shoulder as I drifted off, then jerked awake. Across the water, I heard wordless singing and the sound of people murmuring. Someone is calling me, I thought, struggling to make out the words. Perhaps I dreamed.

In the slow swell of dawn, the sea stretched before us like time, large enough to swallow all history, legend, desire, imagination. I felt the burden of my own story floating away, as if I had rolled up yesterday's fear like parchment, tucked it into a bottle, and sent it off on some other current, not knowing who might read it and understand. We sailed on an ocean awash in the stories of all those who came before us in cedar canoes, sloops of war, merchant schooners, steamers, freighters, fishing boats, dories. In the ghostly light, they moved with us—the Tlingit Indians, the Russian, British, and American explorers, the seafarers and traders, settlers and sailors.

I had studied charts with creases worn soft as flannel, read history and folklore, and now I felt us slipping by secret harbors where bear hunters lived and foreign sailors sought refuge. I peered at reefs where ships foundered, and their passengers with them. We passed abandoned Tlingit forts, lost villages, and all the unmarked places where Natives found marble for polishing wood and stone carvings, or raked up green ribbons of kelp pearled with herring roe, or set halibut hooks carved with human faces down at the bottom of the sea.

Sorrow and loss washed up along these shores, too. The wind pushed us beyond islands where fox farms rot into the forest, past the crooked inlet where a cross marks the place where mother and child drowned, away from the killing rock where Tlingits sacrificed slaves for potlatches.

During our journey, history crested in wave after wave, ebbing into myth, dissolving into time like handfuls of salt tossed into the sea. There were ways to mark our passage, methods of triangulation and calculation that could reveal exactly where we were. There were chronicles that could fix us squarely in the flow of events. I preferred to let the metronome of tides measure out the journey.

In the storm's wake, sunny skies brought air so still that for two days we drifted becalmed and fell still farther behind the race leaders. The slightest breeze wrinkling across the water provoked *Lyric*'s crew into a frenzy. They raised the filmy spinnaker to make a kind of sail called a drifter, a silken square so fine it captured any exhalation. Light glowed through the cloth like rays through stained glass. We slipped from one rippled patch of water to another, craving motion, no matter how meager. Ghosting, the sailors called it.

The change in weather was not received well by the sailors. They languished in a mental doldrums, cross because we had mired in dead air. They quarreled good-naturedly about which sail to try next, what we should have done at the starting line, which shift was more skilled, whose boat would win. They cursed the winds, their luck, each other. They rarely spoke of themselves, or of anything besides sailing. Their ordinary existence was stranded on the other side of the storm.

I left some part of myself behind, too. The race no longer mattered to me, nor did the article I was charged with writing. My notes grew ever more cryptic with the kind of sightings and observations that would fill the log of someone lost at sea: "Wind slight. Nursed spinnaker along for three hours." Or: "Halyard's jammed. Captain went up in bosun's chair." I felt pleasantly doomed, but *Lyric*'s sailors never gave up. If they could have paddled the boat with hands and feet, they would have. They drank canned beer, and adjusted ropes and rigging, and imagined all the ways they could still win. I dangled my feet over the side and spit at my wavering shadow. The spit moved faster than we did.

I supposed they had fiercer hearts than I. I liked not being afraid. I liked these long hours of reflected heat and light. I was becalmed, too, as if I had entered some strange latitude where false tranquility stills all desire and motion. But fear remained something I could taste on my lips, a briny, bitter tang I could lick from my skin. Some people seek a sense of peace in Alaska, but fear binds me to this landscape—fear of what I might find or lose, fear of what might find or lose me, out here where everything seems familiar and foreign, all at once. Alaska is big enough to cradle every true fear and hope we can bear. Why else would I have been out there, far from every safe harbor I've ever known?

For hours I studied the impassive shoreline of Admiralty Island looming like an undiscovered continent to starboard. Through binoculars I peered at reticulated beaches, bays folded into ciphers, the toothy jaws of mountains clapped against the sky. Thick, deep forest draped the slopes, and sometimes the green scent of spruce and hemlock trees enveloped us. Knowing that brown bears and deer roamed the shoreline just beyond sight, I felt their eyes upon us. If I stepped ashore the enormous island, the forest would have swallowed me as surely as the ocean.

All day long, creatures flew or swam past on their own unknowable journeys. Harbor porpoises inscribed perfect arcs. Ravens flapped overhead, every stroke of their black, black wings thunderous in the quiet. For once they said nothing and merely cocked their heads to see us clinging to flotsam. A few hundred yards away, two humpback whales fanned scalloped flukes before diving. A sea lion rolled past, turning brimming eyes toward us, calling in a garbled tongue that unsettled me.

I shielded my face from the sun's painful light and gazed into mossy green depths, trying to picture the underwater landscape we passed over like a small cloud casting shadows. Schools of fingerlings flashed and twisted in eerie unison. Orange, globular jellyfish contracted and expanded like lungs. Rafts of brown rockweed and strips of bull kelp threatened to entangle us. I leaned over too far, and my sunglasses slid off my face and spiraled into darkness.

On the third morning we passed Yasha Island, a tiny speck that marked the entrance to Chatham Strait on the west flank of Admiralty. Bald eagles owned the island; two score perched in spruce trees or hunkered on the rocks. Suddenly, a sailor shouted and pointed. An eagle plummeted to the water's surface to snatch at something, but something snatched it. The bird struggled, wings smashing and beating as it sank below the surface. We watched, but the eagle did not reappear. The sailors wondered what could seize such a powerful bird. I pictured the eagle soaring underwater, bubbles trailing from its feathers as it descended.

At night, when all aspects of land, sea, and sky merged, splashings and murmurings and gurglings became urgent mysteries. I expected fabulous sea creatures to rise thrashing from below and crush us in their beaks, tentacles, jaws. Decades ago, at the junction of Chatham and Peril straits, two Juneau men of impeccable reputation claimed they spotted a sea serpent three hundred feet long gliding in the water. They peppered the greenish blue monster with gunfire, and it sank, writhing. The men waited for its carcass to float but returned to Juneau with nothing but legend. It was not enough to see a monster; they had to own it, too.

I had no need to invent dangers. It was enough to think of unmarked reefs, sudden storms, collisions with other vessels. I had no need to invent dangers, but I did, in those smothering moments before exhaustion dragged me into unconsciousness. And when the fantastic did appear, when humpback whales snorted and heaved around the boat, I floated so far away in sleep that my companions could not call me back.

So we drifted, suspended on the cusp between heaven and sea, sea and earth, between what is above and what is below.

On the fifth day, the wind rose. We saw it coming in the way the seas gathered in a black line along the horizon, like the shadow of an eclipse racing toward us. For a moment, I was afraid. Not another storm. But then I realized how much I craved wind and motion after the long, silent hours. No worse fate for sailors than stillness.

We leapt about, yanking ropes, raising sails, making the ship ready. Waves arrived first, smacking against the hull. Then wind rolled over the boat, strumming the rigging, billowing the canvas, infusing us with a blue desire. Silence fell behind as the bow hissed and sails hummed. *Lyric* quickened. This was what she was made for.

When the sailors felt sated by wind, they urged me to take the helm, to understand their complicated joy. Already they knew that despite their longing and skill, they would not win this race. They could afford to be generous. You are ready, they told me.

I did not steer the boat; I gave myself over to a physics of intuition. Through my hands, I discovered the invisible place where the boat bound together wind and sea and glided along the seam it created with each moment. Air surged around me, and finally pierced me.

And when, too soon, the wind faltered, sails fluttered and fell limp, and the boat subsided, the world settled into an unfortunate equilibrium. I realized that most of the time, I think too much. We sail in search of terror and ecstasy, the sailor said, and he was right.

In Southeast Alaska, there exist more bays, more inlets, more islands than you can imagine. As one of the last blank spaces on eighteenth-century maps, the archipelago became a promising destination for those making their imperial voyages of discovery. Three times Spanish mariners stepped ashore to claim this territory for their crown. Once, they had barely returned to their ship when they saw the Tlingits dragging away the large white cross the Spaniards had just erected to signify possession and benediction of the New World by the Old.

As the outlines of land and sea took shape on charts, others followed. Traders swept through, exchanging trinkets for furs. Capt. George Vancouver surveyed the coastline inch by inch, searching for the Northwest Passage. He scattered like party favors the names of sovereigns, relatives, and people worth flattering: Seymour Canal, Stephens Passage, Chatham Strait, and hundreds of others. The Russians took what was never theirs and sold it to the Americans. The Americans sent soldiers, missionaries, tourists. For a long while, the Tlingits resisted these various occupations, and many still do.

In Southeast Alaska, there exist more beaches, more mountains, more secrets than I can ever know. How many others before me impaled themselves against these rocks, slipped gratefully below the surface, drifted out to sea? I stared at charts, sounded the depths, marked the hazards, and still I had to accept the rapture of the deep, a darkness I could never penetrate, a chaos I will never control. I didn't want to look into the abyss, and I couldn't help but look. I relinquished the useless fantasy of possession, realizing there is only surrender. This is how the lost lighthouse keeper must have felt as he floated toward his destiny.

At midnight on our last night at sea, I apprenticed myself to air. I lay flat against the foredeck, each hand wrapped around a rope that controlled an edge of the drifter. The sail spread above me, slight as a whisper, radiantly paned in summer twilight. A minnow of air wriggled over the boat. I cast the drifter like a gentle net. The cloth trembled, luffed. I teased the ropes that leashed the sail that held the air. The boat answered. All along my body, I sensed it stirring below me. We ghosted.

For hours I submerged myself in this simple task, anticipating the breeze, gathering and easing the sail in response. I breathed through my hands. Remembering the storm, I finally understood that the sailors did not fight the wind. They embraced it. They shaped the boat and themselves to it.

The sailors said nothing to me. I was in another place, and in that place, I did not need their help or their words. A cruise ship steamed by to port, glowing like a chandelier, and I barely glanced. Nothing seemed so filled with light as that sail. The sky deepened into violet clarity, but I refused to be swallowed. The sail, the wind, the rasp of rope against my palms—this seemed enough.

Then, a humpback whale moaned. It pealed like a clapper struck against the dark bell of the ocean. It was a foghorn, a tuning fork, the purest note that harmonizes longing and fulfillment. It was the edge of the world. I fell.

A Man Made Cold by the Universe

BEFORE WE STARTED OUR SMALL JOURNEY to the place where Christopher McCandless died, I wondered whether we should travel on foot rather than by snowmachine. It was mid-April, probably the last weekend before the sketchy snow would melt and the river ice would sag and crack. If we waited a few weeks, we could hike the Stampede Trail to the abandoned bus where his body was found in 1992. Wouldn't it seem more real, more authentic somehow, if we retraced his journey step by step?

No, I thought. This is not a spiritual trek. I refuse to make this a pilgrimage. I will not make his journey my own.

And so we set off on the tundra, snowmachines skirling across a thin layer of hard snow. The five of us moved quickly, each following the other westward through the broad valley. To the south, clouds wisped across the white slopes that barricade Denali National Park and Preserve. Denali itself was a phantom presence on the horizon. I wore ear protectors to dull the grinding noise of the engines. When the sun burned through, we turned our faces toward it gratefully, unzipped our parkas, peeled away fleece masks. It had been a long winter—warmer than most in Interior Alaska, but even so each day was filled more with darkness than with light.

We kept on, the only motion against a landscape that seemed still and perfect in its beauty. It was the kind of day where you could think about McCandless and wonder about all the ways that death can find you in such a place, and you can find death. And then a few minutes later, you'd look out across the valley, admiring the way the spruce-covered hills swell against the horizon, and you might think, "Damn, I'm glad to be alive in Alaska."

A few summers ago I rode in a shuttle van from Fairbanks to the park with a group of vacationers and backpackers. As we left town, the driver began an impromptu tour of the final days of McCandless, a 24-year-old who had hitchhiked to Alaska in April 1992, looking for a place to enter the wilderness. The van driver pointed out a bluff near Gold Hill Road: the last place McCandless had camped in Fairbanks. He talked about the purity of McCandless's desire to test himself against nature. He slowed as we passed the Stampede Road, the place where a Healy man had dropped off McCandless so the young man could begin his journey, ignoring all offers of help except for a pair of rubber boots. He did not take a map. In the van, people whispered to each other and craned their necks to peer at the passing landmarks.

McCandless had hiked about twenty-two miles along the trail before stopping at a rusting Fairbanks city bus left there in the 1960s by roadbuilders creating a route from the highway to the Stampede Mine, near the park boundary. His only sources of food were a .22 rifle and a ten-pound bag of rice. In the back of an Athabascan plant lore book, he scribbled brief and often cryptic entries. In July he tried to leave but apparently was turned back by the roiling Teklanika River. He did not know enough to search for a braided crossing. By August, he was in trouble. A note tacked to the bus pleaded for help from any passerby: "I am injured, near death, and too weak to hike out of here," it said in part. In early September, hunters found his body shrouded in a sleeping bag inside the bus. He had been dead for more than two weeks. Although he had tried to eat off the land, and had even succeeded in killing small animals and a moose, he had starved, an unpleasant and unusual way to die in America these days.

The strange manner of his death made McCandless infamous in Alaska as authorities tried to puzzle out his story. The 1993 *Outside* magazine article by Jon Krakauer, followed by the 1996 best-selling book *Into the Wild*, made him famous everywhere else.

The van driver was maybe in his early thirties, mild and balding. As he drove and talked, he held up a copy of Krakauer's book, a sympathetic and compelling portrait of McCandless. The driver confided that he kept the book with him always because he felt close to the dead man.

"I understand his wanting to come here and go into the wild," the driver said. He, too, had attended Emory University, and he and his wife had recently moved to Anchorage in search of whatever it is people want when they come to Alaska.

In a van full of out-of-state vacationers, the driver felt safe criticizing the response of Alaskans to the story of McCandless. "They called him a young fool who deserved what he got. There was not a positive letter to the editor written about Chris McCandless. It went on for days." He checked our reactions in the rearview mirror. "It was pretty chilling to read."

We do talk about McCandless in Alaska. We talk about him a lot. We can't help ourselves. Mostly the discussion is in response to the book, and mostly it is not favorable because of the way McCandless stars as a romantic hero. Krakauer described McCandless as searching for something beyond his privileged but disappointing middle-class existence:

> It would be easy to stereotype Christopher McCandless as another boy who felt too much, a loopy young man who read too many books and lacked even a modicum of common sense. But the stereotype isn't a good fit. McCandless wasn't some feckless slacker, adrift and confused, racked by existential despair. To the contrary: His life hummed with meaning and purpose. But the meaning he wrested from existence lay beyond the comfortable path. McCandless distrusted the value of things that came easily. He demanded much of himself—more, in the end, than he could deliver.

Many Alaskans take a simpler view. They think the entire meaning of his death was this: he made some dumb-ass decisions, and he died. Others believe he secretly wanted to die; why else would he have made the puzzling choices he did? A few say he was mentally ill; one Anchorage columnist insists that McCandless was clearly schizophrenic. And still others say he died because he was arrogant and prideful, because he didn't honor the power of the land, because he didn't have the humility to observe and ask questions and think.

Nevertheless, because McCandless starved to death in the wilderness—or what many people conceive of as wilderness—by some strange transmogrification he has become a cult hero. Web sites preserve high school and college essays analyzing *Into the Wild*, which is popular on reading lists everywhere and frequently seen in the hands of people touring the state. *The Milepost*, the most detailed road guide in Alaska, now mentions the site: "If you've read *Into the Wild* and want to visit the memorial at the bus, locals advise it is a long hike in from the end of Stampede Road and you have to cross the Savage and Teklanika Rivers." A composer named Cindy Cox wrote a piece meant to convey musically the dying man's states of mind—fear, joy, acceptance, et cetera. A young outdoorsman I know, Joseph Chambers, says that among his friends a new phrase has emerged: "pulling a McCandless." A person who pulls a McCandless may be trying to test himself or to find himself, Chambers explained, or he may be on a fool's mission, risking his life and causing pain to others while recklessly searching for something that may have been meaningless or stupid all along.

And then there are the pilgrims, the scores and scores of believers who, stooped beneath the weight of their packs and lives, walk that long Stampede Trail to see the place where McCandless died, and never take a step beyond.

For two hours we rode along the rim of the shallow valley. Heat from the engines warmed our hands. We followed a trail used by dog mushers and snowmachiners; here and there other trails looped to the north or south, disappearing into the crease and fold of hills scored evenly with black spruce forests like an old woodblock print. We had barely beaten spring. Along low ridges, the packed trail wound across the ground as solidly as a boardwalk, passing russet scraps of tundra patched by snow. A Healy woman named Connie led most of the time because she knew the way. The others in the group were my friends Kris, Joe, and Charles. Charles, a photographer, came along to document the bus and to make tasteless jokes. Kris and Joe live just outside the park. Joe had visited the site shortly after the body was discovered, and Kris, a freelance writer, covered the McCandless story when it first broke in Alaska. She's the one who told me that people had been visiting the bus like it was Jim Morrison's grave in Paris.

The September weekend that hikers and hunters discovered McCandless's body swaddled in his sleeping bag, I happened to be at nearby Denali National Park on an assignment with a newspaper photographer, but an early snowstorm closed the park road, and the city editor asked us instead to check out sketchy reports of someone found dead in the bus. We'd ventured into the makeshift hunting community that forms each year on the Stampede Road to see if anyone would rent or loan us an all-terrain vehicle the next day, but the sudden heavy snow discouraged everybody we asked from risking their four-wheelers with a couple of strangers. The next day Alaska State Troopers retrieved the man's body with a helicopter, along with cryptic notes he'd jotted chronicling the passage of 113 days.

Though eager as any reporter to break such an unusual story, the notion of seeing a dead body didn't appeal to me, and I was mildly relieved we had failed to reach the bus at the time. What interested me now was why so many people could not let McCandless go, the way they insisted on recapitulating his mysterious journey—not toward death but toward some kind of enlightenment—by visiting such a grim relic.

Now and then we rode by other trails looping across the snow, and an hour into our trip, two snowmachiners passed us before we reached the Teklanika River. They were friends of Joe's on their way northward to fix an off-road-tracked vehicle that had broken a fuel line during a fall moose hunt. Their trail curved across a distant ridge, and I admired their ease and confidence roaming around out here, where machines can break down or dogs can run away and the walk home will be long and troublesome. You couldn't call it the middle of nowhere; the Stampede Trail has been mapped for decades. Still, you'd want to know what you're doing, so as not to make your next public appearance in a newspaper headline or as another statistic.

The Teklanika River ice had not yet softened, and we crossed its smooth expanse without trouble, just below where it emerges from a gulch. We cruised through Moose Alley, dipped into the forest, wound across the beaver ponds, and rose along an alder-thick ridgeline. Occasionally moose tracks postholed the snow. I tried to imagine hiking here in the summer, calling out to bears and waving away mosquitoes.

We rounded a bend and suddenly there was bus 142, hollow-eyed and beat up, the most absurd thing you could imagine encountering in this open, white space. Faded letters just below the side windows read, "Fairbanks City Transit System." The derelict bus seemed so familiar because we had seen its picture many times in newspapers and on the jacket of Krakauer's book. For decades it had served as a hunting camp and backcountry shelter, a corroding green-and-white hull of civilization transplanted to a knoll above the Sushana River. Now it was haunted real estate.

We turned off the snowmachines and stood stretching in the sunshine and the kind of quiet that vibrates. A trash barrel, a fire grill, plenty of footprints, and frozen dog shit provided evidence of passing dogsleds and snowmachines. A wire chair leaned against the bus, and I wondered how many people had posed there for photographs. The bus made me uneasy, and I was glad to be there with friends. It must have sheltered many people over the years who came to shoot and drink and close themselves up against the night.

Kris and I squeezed through a gap in the jammed bus door and climbed in. It was warm enough to remove hats and gloves while we looked around, though an occasional draft swept through the broken windows. A bullet hole had pierced the windshield on the driver's side.

The bus was littered with junk and messages referring to McCandless's death, which seemed to bring out the earnestness of a Hallmark card in visitors who had scratched sayings into the rusted ceilings and walls. "Fulfill Your Dreams, Nothing Feels Better" and "Stop Trying to Fool Others As the Truth Lies Within" and "The Best Things in Life Are Free." Scattered among the needles and twigs on the floor were bizarre artifacts: frayed hanks of rope, a mayonnaise jar lid, a camp shower bag, playing cards. The driver's seat was missing, but downy grouse feathers lined crannies in the dashboard. "Keep This Place Clean You Human Pigs," someone had etched.

A few liquor bottles—big gulps remaining of the Jack Daniel's and the Yukon Jack—crowded a small stand. Stowed beneath were worn Sorel boots and pairs of filthy jeans, one set patched crudely with scraps of a green wool army blanket. Were these the jeans mentioned in the book? Hard to believe they were still here considering that locals joke about dismantling the bus and selling it on eBay. Still, it was a creepy moment.

A stovepipe lurched from a small barrel woodstove and poked through the roof. A green tent fly covered the rusted springs of a twin-size mattress. And here was the disturbing part: the bed lodged sideways against the bus's rear, mattress stained, strawlike stuffing exposed, the remnants of the cover torn and shredded. That's where his body was found.

On the wall beside the bed was a brass plaque left by his family. It read:

> *Christopher Johnson McCandless. "Alex." 2/68–8/92. Chris, our beloved son and brother, died here during his adventurous travels in search of how he could best realize God's great gift of life. With his final message, "I have had a happy life and thank the Lord. Goodbye and may God Bless All," we commend his soul to the world. The McCandless Family. 7/93*

McCandless had been introducing himself as "Alex" at least since he'd graduated from college in 1990 and started his restless prowl westward, and inward. When he discovered the bus on his trek into Alaska's backcountry, he'd written a message referring in the third person to an "aesthetic voyager whose home is the road," a man on a *final adventure*, ready to *battle to kill the false being within* and finish a *spiritual pilgrimage*—his words—and he signed it "Alexander Supertramp." The family's memorial plaque acknowledges the existence of the two of them, Christopher and Alexander. But which one did the dying, there at the end?

Three notebooks sat on the plywood table. They included a three-ring binder protecting a photocopy of Krakauer's original magazine article with the blaring headline "Lost In the Wild." It was a Monty Python moment when someone pointed out an unrelated title on the cover: "Are you too thin? The case for fat." This kind of humor is one reason why Alaskans fear dying ridiculously: the living are so cruel to the foolish dead. It's a way of congratulating ourselves on remaining alive.

Kris and I began flipping through the steno notebooks, which had been filled with comments by visitors, the way people write in logbooks left in public cabins or guest books set out at art galleries. The chronology began with the July 1993 visit by McCandless's parents. His mother wrote:

> *Sonny boy, it's time to leave. The helicopter will soon arrive. I wondered briefly if it would be hard to enter your last home. The wonderful pictures you left in your final testament welcomed me in and I'm finding it difficult to leave, instead. I can appreciate joy in your eyes reported by your self-portraits. I, too, will come back to this place. Mom.*

These heartfelt words were followed by a single sentence from Krakauer himself: "Chris—Your memory will live on in your admirers."

"Oh, gag," Kris said—referring not to Krakauer but to the notion of "admirers."

Kris is not what you would call romantic about the wilderness. She and Joe are among the most competent Alaskans I know. They hunt, guide river trips, paddle white water all through Alaska and Canada, and travel frequently in the backcountry. In March, they had wanted to catch some of the Iditarod Trail Sled Dog Race, so they'd snowmachined from their house near McKinley Village through the uninhabited midsection of Alaska to Rainy Pass, winter-camping along the three-hundred-mile route. I was embarrassed about my modest survival gear when I saw how well-rigged their machines were with snowshoes, a come-along, and other useful equipment compactly stowed. To people like them, the adulation of McCandless is just one more reason to stay in sensible old Alaska.

Joe clumped into the bus and read Krakauer's note in a flat voice. "Your memory will live on in your admirers? Huh."

Beneath the bed was a small blue suitcase, a Starline, the kind your grandmother might have taken on weekend trips. The lid was busted off the hinges. McCandless's mother had filled it with survival gear and left it, and over the years other people have removed things or added to it. Joe dragged the suitcase out, plopped it on the bed, and called out an inventory as he sorted through the jumble of things useful and not, beginning with a crumpled silver survival blanket: "The Jiffy Pop tinfoil thing.

Look right here: saltwater taffy. Holy Bible. Cheesecloth. A map saying 'You are here. Walk this way out to get food.'"

He was joking about that. When he finished poking through the suitcase, he went outside so Charles could take his picture posing by the famous bus with a can of Spam in his left hand. "That's almost bad luck," Connie said quietly, and I had to agree.

Kris and I took turns reading aloud comments left by those who started coming the year after Krakauer's book was published. Some were epistles, others aphorisms. The few entries made by Alaskans included the sort of information useful to other backcountry travelers. A Stampede Trail resident wrote a detailed description of how to cross the Teklanika River when it runs high—a problem that had defeated McCandless. Added in pencil was the advice, "Also, there's the park boundary cabin 6 miles away—upstream on the Sushana river. Food there. Don't trash the place."

In May, the first seekers began arriving and recording more intimate thoughts.

"I cried so much I couldn't believe it."

"This bus has a sacred feeling to it and I feel grateful to be able to visit the place where Chris lived and died."

"I'll return next year and try to set myself free again."

"The vibes I felt from the bus made me sit and think for hours. I wasn't able to sleep until I felt every emotion possible: amazed, sadness, wonderment, happiness, and many more . . ."

Charles looked over my shoulder and read. "I wish I could come in here and have an inspirational moment," he said. "I wish my life was Zenned out."

Kris wondered if we were too cynical, and of course we were. We were too cynical to read entry after entry from people looking for meaning in the life and death of a man who had rejected his family, mooched his way across the country, and called himself "Alexander Supertramp" in the third person. I struggled to imagine the emotional currents that had carried people here to this bus, so far from their homes, to honor his memory. Later, a friend who had been born in Alaska and exiled to Maryland for five years tried to explain the overwhelming smallness and sameness to life on the suburban East Coast. Lawn care excited the most interest, she said, only half-joking, so no wonder someone like McCandless seems adventurous and spiritual and inspiring, despite being dead.

Several visitors mentioned that *Into the Wild* had prompted their trips, but the book must have motivated nearly all of the pilgrim, because why else would people attach any significance to the bus? They had come from Europe, California, Alabama, Michigan, Minnesota, Utah, Ontario, North Carolina. One man made the journey after reading a book review while sitting in a doctor's office in Ithaca, New York. "It was then I knew the bus was a place I must visit," he wrote. A fellow from Belgium wrote: "I've come from Europe to follow the footsteps of a 'pilgrim,' as says Krakauer, and I'd almost say a prophet!" He then criticized the materialistic attitude of Alaskans and urged them to read Tolstoy "instead of prostituting their country to tourism."

I laughed at that one, because the Belgian and the others had themselves turned the bus into a perverse tourist destination. They urged each other to protect the vehicle as a memorial, to leave things untouched for future visitors. "His monument and tomb are a living truth whose flame will light the 'way of dreams' in other's lives," someone wrote. It was not hard to imagine that before long visitors would be able to buy T-shirts saying, "I Visited The Bus" or "I Survived Going Into the Wild." In fact, so many people seemed to have found their way out here that an espresso stand didn't seem out of the question.

Astounded by page after page of such writings, we counted the number of people identified in the notebooks. More than two hundred people had trekked to the bus in the eight years since McCandless's death, and that didn't account for those who passed by without comment. Think of that. More than two hundred people, many as inexperienced as McCandless, had hiked or bicycled along the Stampede Trail to the bus. A few, mostly the Alaskans, had driven snowmachines or dogsleds. And every one of them, unlike the unfortunate McCandless, had somehow managed to return safely.

Only one person even vaguely questioned this paradox: "Perhaps we shouldn't romanticize or cananize [sic] him . . . After all, Crane and I walked here in no time at all, so Chris wasn't far from life . . . not really." But then, perhaps unwilling to seem harsh, the writer added, "These questions are in vain. We shouldn't try to climb into another's mind, attempting to know what he thought or felt."

It was Kris who pointed out how many people promised in their comments to call their families as soon as they could:

"Now it's time to go home to the ones I love and help bring truth to the light." So who's to say their journeys were wasted? But I could not help feeling fascinated and repelled by the desire of so many visitors to find profound moral lessons in such a silly death.

"Chris may have fucked up, but he fucked up brilliantly," wrote some graduate students. "Nonetheless, family *and* freedom would have been better."

And on and on.

Among my friends and acquaintances, the story of McCandless makes great after-dinner conversation. Much of the time I agree with the "he had a death wish" camp because I don't know how else to reconcile what we know of his ordeal. Now and then I venture into the "what a dumbshit" territory, tempered by brief alliances with the "he was just another romantic boy on an all-American quest" partisans. Mostly I'm puzzled by the way he's emerged as a hero, a kind of privileged-yet-strangely-dissatisfied-with-his-existence hero.

But it's more complicated than that. I understand his desire to do some good in the world, and I can almost understand why he rejected maps, common sense, conventional wisdom, and local knowledge before embarking on his venture. Occasionally when I hear others make fun of McCandless, I fall quiet. My favorite book growing up was Scott O'Dell's *Island of the Blue Dolphins*, based on a true story about a nineteenth-century Chumash Indian girl who survived for years alone on an island off the California coast. How often I had imagined myself living in that hut of whale bones, catching fish by hand and taming wild dogs for companionship. It's common, this primal longing to connect with a natural world that provides and cradles, that toughens and inspires.

Live here long enough, though, and you'll learn that every moment spent admiring endless vistas or wandering the land is a privilege, accompanied by plenty of other moments evading mosquitoes by the millions, outlasting weather, avoiding giardia, negotiating unruly terrain, and thinking uneasily about the occasional predator. Walking cross-country through alder thickets or muskeg may be the hardest thing you do all year, as you fight against the earth's tendency to grab hold of you for itself.

And of course it's hard to eat out there. A friend who trapped in his youth likens the Bush to a desert, nearly empty of wildlife. One winter he ate marten tendons for days because his food ran out. Read the journal of Fred Fickett, who accompanied Lt. Henry Allen on a fifteen-hundred-mile exploration of the Copper, Tanana, and Koyukuk river valleys; it is the story of hungry men. May 20, 1885: "One of our dogs found a dead goose. We took it from him and ate it." May 22: "Had rotten salmon straight for breakfast. It was so bad that even the Indian dogs wouldn't eat it. May 28: "Had a little paste for breakfast, rotten and wormy meat for dinner, rotten goose eggs and a little rice for supper . . . about ¼ what we needed." May 30: "Indian gave us a dinner of boiled meat from which he had scraped the maggots in handfuls before cutting it up. It tasted good, maggots and all."

There's a reason the Natives sometimes starved in the old days—and they knew what they were doing. There's a reason that many homesteaders and Bush rats collect welfare to supplement hunting and fishing. There's a reason we gather in cities and villages. So many people want to believe that it's possible to live a noble life alone in the wilderness, living entirely off the land—and yet the Native peoples of Alaska know that only by depending upon each other, only by forming a community, does survival become possible.

People have been dying in the wilderness for as long as people have been going into it. There are always lessons to be learned from such sad stories, even lessons as simple as: Don't forget matches, don't sweat in the cold, don't run away from bears. But sometimes there are no learning moments, no explanations. From an account in the *Nome Nugget* of July 30, 1901:

> *The death of George Dean by starvation at the mouth of the Agiapuk River and the narrow escape of his two companions, Thierry and Houston, from the same fate makes a strange story. Without wishing to criticise the survivors, it looks as if they did not make that hustle for life which men should. They were so near the course of navigation that they could hear the voices of men as they passed up and down the river.*

Why didn't they . . . why couldn't they . . . why wouldn't they? And the wise *Nome Nugget* avoids this trap by shrugging away such unanswerables: "But it's a strange country, and strange things happen in it."

In 1930, not far south from the Stampede Road, park rangers found the body of prospector Tom Kenney on a bar of the McKinley River. He had disappeared July 19 after separating from his partner while they searched for a lost gold placer mine. On September 3, searchers discovered Kenney lying on his back with his arms at his side. One shoe was off, and searchers concluded he had been salving his foot, "which would indicate that he had been in his right mind up to the last," the newspaper reported. He must have eaten berries. He had killed and eaten several porcupines. At his final camp, rangers found a large pile of unburned dry wood.

"It is known that Kenney always kept a diary, but as his pockets were not examined before burial it will never be known whether he set down an account of his wanderings or not," the *Alaska Weekly* reported.

You can hear the pain of letting go in the words of a prospector and trapper named Tom O'Brien, who died of scurvy in the summer of 1919 on the Whiting River near Juneau. In the book *The Dangerous North*, historian Ed Ferrell includes O'Brien's diary entries that describe his teeth rattling in his sore gums, his fever, and his aching joints, the effects of which conspired to keep him from collecting water, firewood, and food. Day by day, he ate one meal of unheated rice or potato soup. He weakened, and his mental faculties faded. Finally he realized he was suffering from scurvy, but his relief measures came too late. (A Tlingit friend shook her head upon reading this account; she could not believe that anyone could be so ignorant as to die of scurvy amid the natural providence of Southeast Alaska.) After two months of recording his trials, he left behind a final entry: "Life is dying hard. The heart is strong."

So many ways to die in the north, in manners grand and surprising and sad. A moment's inattention, the proverbial series of small miscalculations that add up to one giant screw-up, delusion about one's abilities, hubris, mental imbalance, plain bad luck—that's all it takes.

For a few weeks one spring, I kept track of news articles reporting outdoor deaths. Over the winter, more than thirty Alaskans died in snowmachine accidents by losing their way in blizzards, falling through ice and drowning, suffocating in avalanches, colliding into each other. An intoxicated man perched on a boat's gunwales fell into the Chena River in downtown Fairbanks when waves rocked the vessel; his body did not emerge for days. Two men suffocated from carbon monoxide poisoning after they brought a charcoal grill into their tent near Chena Hot Springs. Two young kayakers were missing and presumed dead in the Gulf of Alaska. Campers found the bones of an eighteen-year-old soldier who had disappeared while ice fishing near the Knik Arm fifteen years before. And even as searchers looked for a man who had disappeared in the Chugach Mountains came the news that seventy-year-old Dick Cook, an extraordinary woodsman described by John McPhee as the "acknowledged high swami of the river people," had drowned in the Tatonduk, a river he knew intimately. Some days it seemed surprising that people survive the outdoors at all.

And yet there we were, we crude Alaskans, scoffing and making jokes in Fairbanks 142, shaking our heads and posing with cans of Spam. We want it both ways, it seems. We want to impress people and ourselves with scary tales of death defied at every turn, to point out that Alaska is so unforgiving that a person could die just a few miles away from help. And still we scorn those drawn to that mystique, to those poor, foolish slobs who manage to die out of ignorance or stupidity or even bad luck. Perhaps that's because we know that one day—just like that, really—we could so easily become one of those poor, foolish slobs ourselves.

Mindful of the universe of errors that awaited me on my own small excursions, I took to carrying an all-weather notebook into which I'd taped notes reminding myself how to cross rivers, take compass bearings, or program a GPS. It seemed too cautious, but I could never shake a story that Kris had covered when the wasted body of Carl McCunn and his heartbreaking journal were discovered in 1983. He had been dropped off in the Brooks Range in March 1982, figuring to spend a few months taking photographs. He wasn't inexperienced; he'd spent five months alone in these mountains before. But he arranged his plane pickup too vaguely, and no one came looking for him in August. His food dwindled as winter came on, and he was growing desperate when a search plane flew over his camp at the request of worried friends in Fairbanks. Because he didn't know the established signals a person should use, he unintentionally waved the plane off with the ALL OK sign. In November, he stoked the fire with the last of his wood and penned a good-bye note. "They say it doesn't hurt," he wrote before shooting himself in the head with his rifle. I always carry a plastic signal card with me now.

One disquieting thing cannot be addressed by any notes or cheat sheet, but it's important to know. Sometimes I surrender too soon, as if whatever happens out there is inevitable, and so I'll wait a moment too long to grab a shoe snatched away in a boisterous current, or fail to right that tipping boat, or succumb to a chill or a discouragement overtaking me. Those are precisely the moments when a friend has turned back to walk with me, or lunged after that disappearing object, or pulled me from a river or a mood. This is not to say I haven't overcome problems on my own—the black bear that wouldn't stop approaching me the week I spent alone at Glacier Creek, or the fear that nearly swamped me paddling above the waterfall at Plateau Glacier. But there's a truth that comes to all of us, sooner or later. Sometimes your self isn't enough. Sometimes your self can't save you.

Plenty of people can offer advice about how to survive in the wilderness. From a list written by a miner on December 13, 1897:

> *Don't try to go out even 300 yards with wet feet in cold weather. Stop and make a fire.*
> *Don't take a long trip or leave the trail by yourself. Be with someone as much as possible.*
> *Don't try to go too far without eating and always arrange to have something to eat.*
> *Don't believe everything you hear.*
> *Don't for God's sake, let a hungry man pass your cabin.*
> *Don't be stingy, selfish, or crabby.*
> *Don't go out without a piece of candle in your pocket. You can always get a fire with a candle.*

I'd add one more: *Keep moving always.* Canadian author Rudy Wiebe, explaining the Inuit way of understanding dimension in the landscape, writes, "In order to live a human being must move; to live in the Arctic a human being must, generally speaking, move quite a lot to acquire enough food." Keep moving, and it's almost impossible to be lost, they believe. Someone will almost always cross your path. Thus, two teen-age girls from Selawik, lost in a blizzard after snowmachining thirty miles to a basketball game in spring 2001, kept walking. They ate snow, prayed, counted mountains, and walked. They had almost reached home when searchers found them on the sixth day.

Addison Powell, a prospector and explorer, described this motion while he was traveling near the Mentasta Mountains in 1898. One day, after his group stopped to make camp, a young Native boy and girl appeared from the brush. In good English, they explained that they had attended a mission school on the Yukon. When the boy left school to go hunting with his uncle, the girl had followed. She was twelve years old. Powell wrote:

> She had traveled through the forests, along mountain trails and across dangerous rivers, to this lonely spot, living on berries and roots while making the trip. She had made little rafts of dead sticks, bound together with willow withes, and on one of those she had crossed the great Tanana River. With her inborn instinct to follow the proper course, she had watched for the only smoke on the Tokio River, for she had good reasons to believe that it rose from the campfire of her relatives. This child of the wild had accomplished that which not one full-grown white person in a hundred could have done.

Oddarne Skaldebo was such a person. In 1997, Skaldebo, a Norwegian geologist, set off on a solo trek from a remote lake to the village of Koyukuk, seventy-five air miles away on the Yukon River. Skaldebo was following someone, too. His maternal grandfather, a prospector, had vanished in western

Alaska in 1912, and this disappearance had become part of Skaldebo's internal landscape.

Skaldebo, fifty-one years old, was an experienced hiker, well-prepared with maps, a .44 handgun, food. His friends called him "Odd Arnie" because he enjoyed traveling alone. But a week into his trek, he realized he had badly underestimated the difficulty of the soggy terrain. He traveled but a mile a day. (McCandless apparently had planned to walk to the Bering Sea, but after a week he returned to the bus when the hard truths of Alaska's terrain became known to him.)

Still, Skaldebo kept on; he had no choice. His World War II army boots eroded his feet. Temperatures fell as winter crept closer. As his food disappeared, he ate grayling, rosehips, and berries until a snowstorm iced the bushes. He starved.

But as he starved, he walked toward a cabin noted on his map, where he found enough food to recover and push on. He swam across an icy creek because he did not have the strength to search for a crossing. Imagine what it took to plunge into that water, to expose himself to one more life-sapping force. To keep his spirits up, each day he read "The Quitters," a poem by Robert Service ("Just have one more try—it's dead easy to die/It's the keeping-on-living that's hard").

Two miles from Koyukuk, after two months in the Bush, he fell through thin ice on the Koyukuk River and nearly drowned. But the day after searchers gave up on him, he walked into the village, forty pounds lighter and still alive.

"Skaldebo's is a classic northland survival story," a reporter for the *Anchorage Daily News* noted. Skaldebo made mistakes, just as Christopher McCandless did, just as we all have. But

Skaldebo didn't stop moving, and he didn't die, and that's probably why you haven't heard his name.

Occasionally I paused while flipping through the notebooks and looked out a busted window to watch how the midafternoon sun glazed the snow. We needed to return before dark, so I started skimming the entries, my eyes catching only certain words: Peace. Solitude. Meaning.

It was hard work, resisting the longing that rose from the scribbled words. I spent some moments puzzling over this comment written by a man from Ontario: "[Chris] gave his life in exchange for knowledge and his story is his contribution to the world. I feel complete now to put this story behind me as it was on my mind for quite some time."

This may be our oldest, truest survival skill: the ability to tell and to learn from each other's stories, whether from Aesop's fables, quest narratives, Greek mythology, the book of Genesis, office gossip, the wisdom of elders, or made-for-TV movies. In some ways, Alaska is nothing but stories. We have constructed many of our ideas about this place, and about ourselves, from creation stories, gold rush stories, hunting and fishing stories, pioneer stories, family stories, clan stories. Even the animals told tales in the old Story Time, which is long behind us now.

Pay attention to what people say in bars and across dinner tables and around campfires, and often they are really telling survival stories of some sort or another: How I crossed the river, how I lost the trail, how I got my moose, how I fixed my boat, how I left home for the north, how I beat the storm, how I made it through another cold and lonely winter, how I became a true Alaskan. What all these stories mean, though—that's up to you, the listener.

We can't know exactly why Christopher McCandless died. What matters now is what people want to believe about his death. Krakauer hypothesized that toxic seeds of the wild potato plant weakened him, and early test results seemed to support that. But chemists at the University of Alaska Fairbanks further studied wild potato seeds and other plant parts, as well as seeds from the similar-looking wild sweet pea, and their work seemed to eliminate the poisoning theory.

"I would be willing to bet money that neither species had toxic metabolites that would account for the fate of McCandless," chemist Tom Clausen wrote to me in an e-mail. His conclusions had appeared in the *Fairbanks Daily News-Miner* as early as 1997 but never received wide coverage. Clausen added, "I believe McCandless died not from toxic foods but from foolishness. I hate to be so blunt about the dead but he clearly went 'into the wild' unprepared."

A decade after McCandless died, this information finally reached a wider public. Following the 2007 publication of a *Men's Journal* article reporting Clausen's results, Krakauer updated his book to acknowledge the findings. Then he speculated that a poisonous mold growing on plant seeds interfered with McCandless's metabolism and caused slow starvation. A film version of *Into the Wild* also enshrines the notion that McCandless must have been poisoned, that he could not have simply starved. It's more comforting to think that nature tricked him rather than accepting that maybe he fooled himself.

McCandless's biggest mistake may have been his failure to listen to the right stories. He ignored advice about the scarcity of game, the practicalities of bear protection, the importance of maps, the truths of the land. He was too intent on creating the story of himself.

And yet, that story has such power, such meaning for so many people, that they feel drawn—called personally—to travel across the globe and hike the trail all that way to the bus to look for Christopher McCandless, or Alexander Supertramp, or themselves. They endure mosquitoes and rain and tough walking and bad river crossings and the possibility of bears. The burden the pilgrims carry to the bus is so heavy, laden with their frailties and hopes and desires, and with their lives that don't quite satisfy. And when they arrive, they sit in that cold bus and think, and sometimes they cry from loss and longing and relief.

So many of them are young, and they're lost, somehow, just as he was.

It was a long time before I realized that the story of Christopher and Alexander is not the story of someone who planned to live off the land at all. It is the story of someone who hoped to live off himself, to discover the true self who would emerge able to overcome all weaknesses, all fears, all worldly attachments. This is the version that matters to the pilgrims who work so hard to keep his story alive. They don't care whether he could tell the difference between a caribou and a moose or knew anything about crossing rivers. They care that he wanted freedom, intensity, experience. They forget that toward the end of his life, he returned to the first person in his plea for help from any passerby: "I am all alone, this is no joke. In the name of God, please remain to save me." He signed it as Christopher McCandless. Perhaps Alexander Supertramp was gone by then.

The Alaskans who don't get why he didn't bother learning some useful things before his sojourn are those most uncomfortable with the notion that someone would be so unabashedly self-absorbed as to mistake the wilds without for the wilds within. Perhaps we're too embarrassed to admit some other part of the story we secretly tell ourselves, the part in which we were once more like McCandless than we can admit. Perhaps we've learned that you can walk, and walk, and walk in search of someone different than the person you are, only to discover you were there all along, and only you.

As he was dying, McCandless made a portrait of himself propped against the bus. He held up a good-bye note, a smile on his gaunt face, and from this photograph Krakauer concluded that "Chris McCandless was at peace, serene as a monk gone to God." But only McCandless could have known what truth was in his heart, there at the end. All we can say is that whoever he was, he's not that person anymore. Jon Krakauer made a story about him, by way of telling his own, and every pilgrim since his death has shaped him into something different as well. I'm doing it right now, too.

For many Alaskans, the problem is not necessarily that Christopher McCandless attempted what he did. Most of us came here in search of something, didn't we? Haven't we made our own embarrassing mistakes? But of all the stories in Alaska—stories about Raven and Koatlekanee and Oddarne Skaldebo and the two girls from Selawik—this is the one that people buy in airports and read on the way to their Alaskan adventure. This is the one that makes people walk out to the bus, cry a little, and think they've learned something about the north. This is the one that fools people into thinking they understand something about McCandless and themselves.

We can't afford to take his story seriously because it doesn't say much a careful person doesn't already know about desire and survival. The lessons are so obvious as to be laughable: Look at a map. Take some food. Know where you are. Listen to people who are smarter than you. Be humble. Go on out there—but it won't mean much unless you come back.

This is what bothers me—that McCandless failed so harshly, so sadly, and yet so *famously* that his death has come to symbolize something admirable. His unwillingness to see Alaska for what it really is has somehow become the story so many people associate with this place, a story so hollow you can almost hear the wind blowing through it. His death was not a brilliant fuck-up. It was not even a terribly original fuck-up. It was just one of the more recent and more point-less fuck-ups.

At 3 p.m., after we'd read through the notebooks, taken our silly and disrespectful photographs, and eaten our lunches, we climbed back on our snowmachines and left. We rode against the wind as the light softened and dimmed all around. It grew colder, but it was still a good day to be outside, with spring on its way. I could feel fond about winter, now that it was dwin-dling. What I really wanted was to keep going beyond the bus, across the Sushana River and maybe down into the park.

Following our tracks home reminded me of a story reported in the newspapers the previous winter about a man who had disappeared during a snowmachine trip between two villages on the Yukon-Kuskokwim Delta. The chances of him surviving the frigid coastal winds seemed slight, but for weeks people reported seeing him on the tundra and in the village. The figure ran away when approached. Eventually the man's body was found facedown in the snow. He could not have survived more than two days, the coroner said. Yet people had seen him wandering around the delta, hiding among homes in the village, unable to move on. The Yup'ik elders explained that he was *cillem quellra*. Rough translation: "Made cold by the universe." He was mired in the thin place where two worlds rub together.

Poor Christopher McCandless, entombed by the tributes of his pilgrims, forever wandering between the world he wanted and the world that exists, still trapped by other people's desires to make him something he is not—which is why he came out here in the first place. People think they see him and feel him, there at the bus. Perhaps he is indeed within our vision, but he is not within our reach.

Too late he learned that the hard part isn't walking toward the wilderness to discover the meaning of life. The hard part is returning from the consolations of nature and finding meaning anyway, a meaning lodged within the faithfulness of our ordinary lives, in the plain and painful beauty of our ordinary days.

Some day, I told myself, I might return. I'd do what few people do anymore, which is to pass by that junky old bus with only a sidelong glance and see what else is out there.

Approaching the Mountain

WHAT NO ONE SAYS about adventuring is that you never know when the gods may finally address you. You don't get to decide when some oracle will open its pink, cavernous mouth and deliver prophecies that seem puzzling in the moment, and later, in the deepest hollow of night, so true. And isn't that why you undertook your journey—so you could earn wisdom, or receive it, one or the other?

So you aren't allowed to ignore revelation, even when it comes in the guise of Ed and Gladys of San Diego, two stout, middle-aged people who have dressed in bright raiments for their very first dinner in Denali National Park, here at the Kantishna Roadhouse. Ed and Gladys were the roadhouse's first customers of the tourist season, and they paid $560 a night for the privilege of staying here because the roadhouse is one of the few lodgings allowed within the park. When they walked by us, smiling distantly, the roadhouse naturalist, Eric, said to them, "Here's some folks you'll be interested in talking with." He described how my two friends and I had just hiked thirty hard miles into the park from the Bearpaw River. Ed and Gladys could see how the miles showed on our dirty clothes, how our backpacks tilted against their ludicrous weight. Eric explained that we were walking to the foot of Denali as a way of retracing a journey made by Judge James Wickersham in 1903, when he attempted to be the first to summit the fabled peak. I liked how Eric made our trip sound as if it were an accomplishment already.

Ed and Gladys nodded politely, making "Mmmm-hmmm" sounds, and Gladys said, by way of exchanging adventure stories, "I'm sick. I'm nauseous and I have diarrhea."

Most visitors to Alaska like talking about their travels, not hearing about other people's. I feel the same way, so I wasn't exactly paying attention as Gladys and Ed took turns describing how the flight to Kantishna in the bush plane was a little rough, that they left their RV in Fairbanks, that they came by way of Dawson, where they sampled a Sourtoe cocktail, a famous tourist concoction featuring someone's frostbitten big toe steeped in spirits. Still, you'd think they would want to hear more about *our* trip. They could have asked a few courteous questions: See any bears? Fall in any rivers? Lose heart? But they didn't.

After relating their various travels, to which we responded politely, "Mmmm-hmmm," they said good-bye and headed for the dining room, Ed cloaked in a Hawaiian shirt, Gladys's swirly skirt and hippie beads swaying as she moved.

Then Ed turned back. He said, "That's interesting, fol-lowing in people's footsteps. You can never do that exactly, you know."

And Gladys added, over her shoulder, "You can never have their same thoughts. You can never know what it was like to be them at that time."

I knew that. I did. But does it take a pair of California tourists to point out the futility of this quest, the thinness of my desire? They heard nothing of our wanderings across the tundra, the struggle through muskeg when game trails evaporated, the trudge through rain and wind, that skittish dash across a thawing ice bridge, this weariness inside and out. They didn't care that we surrendered months of planning on the first day of hiking. It did not matter to them whether I ever stood at the foot of Denali, feeling whatever it is I think I ought to feel.

That night, lying in a wall tent, woozy from fatigue and beer, I realized why Ed and Gladys, the seers of San Diego, annoyed me so. It wasn't because they didn't understand why I'd make this journey. It was because I didn't.

In Fairbanks I lived in a ridgetop cabin, and every day I drove past a scenic overlook where teenagers gathered to smoke and neck, construction workers ate lunch, truck drivers idled, and tourists videotaped the view. Every one of them was look-ing for Denali. Sometimes I wondered how many thousands of times I looked beyond the stubby buildings of downtown Fairbanks and across the serpentine shine of the Tanana River until my eyes rested on the vague horizon, where sometimes the mountain was visible, lumpish as a bowl of melting ice cream, and sometimes it was not.

I first saw the mountain when I was eight and my family lived in the park for the summer. Once the family drove the thin, dusty road all the way to Wonder Lake, not quite thirty miles from the mountain itself. My fishing line zipped through the dark water, teasing phantom fish. Mosquitoes rose from the marshy lake rim as we roasted hot dogs on peeled willow sticks. On the road home a copper fox begged Cheetos from passersby. My mother clicked her tongue and said, "Poor thing, her kits will starve," and my father snapped a picture anyway.

But about the mountain, I don't remember a thing. It must have seemed so large, so abstract and remote, as to be unseeable and unknowable, something like the future, or maybe death.

Decades later, I studied James Wickersham's account of the first recorded attempt to climb Denali, trying to fit the published version against the loopy scrawl in his diary. His noble whimsy is so appealing. He's middle-aged, an ambitious Tacoma lawyer appointed to oversee an ungovernable chunk of territorial Alaska. But look how he has taken to it: dogsledding along his circuit, moose hunting in the fall, moving his court to the new gold camp of Fairbanks in spring 1903 to fashion it into a respectable town. Within days, he decides to attempt the mountain and assembles a group to accompany him. They'll take a steamer downriver as far as they can, walk to the mountain, and begin climbing. Why not? Nobody else has.

It never occurs to him how ridiculous it is that a judge, a mule skinner, a court stenographer, and two hunters would attempt to climb the largest peak in North America. Those were the times they lived in. People could do just about anything then. They could drive dog teams hundreds of miles to the next gold camp through weather so cold it would kill whatever didn't keep moving. They could raise towns in the wilderness, watch them burn, and rebuild them within days. They could walk from the coast of Alaska inland as far as their legs would take them, halted only by crippling inexperience, bad decisions, or poor luck.

To Wickersham, Denali was the most interesting thing on the horizon:

> *The oftener one gazes upon its stupendous mass, the stronger becomes the inclination to visit its base and spy out the surroundings. From the moment we reached the Tanana valley the longing to approach it had been in my mind; now the opportunity was at hand. Could we blaze a new trail into a distant and unknown wilderness of forest and mountain, extend geographic knowledge and possibly aid in the development of a new mining camp? After much cogitation, I began to organize a party for the trip.*

All those grand urges: *blazing, extending, developing.* I shared only one: *longing.* Somehow the idea occurred that by walking toward the mountain every day for a couple of weeks, following Wickersham's route, I'd have a finer understanding of what it means to explore, to discover something, if only the sense of an earlier time when everything began with "un": untouched, unconquered, unknown.

Wickersham wanted to climb Denali. I wanted only to see it as if for the first time.

My husband wouldn't come. He doesn't like tramping around the backcountry. *Not as much as you do, anyway,* he conceded.

It's hard to explain such compulsions. What bullshit, I'd think, the way everything has to be justified, understood, reasoned. Because there's no good explanation for dragging everyone across this most difficult terrain, when I'm *not even going to climb the mountain.* Why would I? I hate to be cold. After all those winters in Fairbanks, all those thirty-below days trawling through an inland sea of cold, why surrender one whole spring to mountaineering, which is nothing more than distilled and vertical winter? Let's be honest: I don't have that many springs to spare. I don't know the first thing about crevasses and ice picks and ropes. I'm afraid of crossing glacial rivers, much less glaciers.

I shrugged when I told people: *Because it'll be fun. Because I've always wanted to.* When, at last, a few others said they would go, I never asked them why. Isn't the doing of it enough? Though you can't be sure until you've done it.

The mountain was nowhere in sight the moment we began our journey, whenever that was. Perhaps it was when my companions and I, leaning against gear and gas barrels stacked into a twenty-one-foot metal riverboat, left the banks of the Chena River on a morning late in May. The moment we turned from waving to family and friends and gazed down the river, facing forward, counting off the waterways that lead toward the mountain: the placid Chena, the broad and burly Tanana, the winding Kantishna, the narrowing waters of the clear Bearpaw.

Two-hundred-something river miles had to be crossed before we could take a step, miles that uncoiled across the flats as the boat ticked around each bend and tocked the other way. The pyramid of Chitsia Mountain swung across the horizon like a pendulum, marking the place where Wickersham began his trek. Along the banks, moose stood among the alders, sometimes with a chestnut-colored newborn tucked beneath. Northering geese flew low enough that an eye glittered when they cocked their heads to study us. One of the men, the one who grew up in this territory, taught me to distinguish from all the shapes that once said "duck" and now said "wigeon" or "merganser." At night a pair of tundra swans called from across the river, their breath reedy and sonorous, and it seemed fair to think they, too, were glad to be back in the country.

Perhaps the journey began as my two hiking companions and I stood at the threshold of the spruce forest, just beyond the place where the boat could travel no farther in the shallowing river. Already my shoulders stooped beneath that heavy, heavy pack. That quickening within—I knew this was the step that mattered, because once you've taken it, you can only keep going. I pushed into the alder thickets, and they pushed back, and now we moved into a green, secret world hidden from the sky, from the river.

We followed paths eased into the earth by bears, wolves, moose, and the smaller beasts that live here. They were most interested in shadowing the curvy river, and so we did, too, taking the long way to the mountain. There were no shortcuts, no mild-mannered trails to beckon us forward with friendly arrows, no guideposts to count. There was no mountain to fix our gaze upon. There was only this: one step, and then another.

On that first difficult day, I realized I am not one of those people of whom it is said, after something terrible happens to them outdoors, "She died doing what she loved." I did not want to die out here at all.

And what was it that I loved about this, exactly? Not the leg-burning struggle, the constant halo of mosquitoes, the way alders tugged at the backpack and dragged across my face and scraped my hands. Not the sight of that scat dumped on the game trail, and the flat conversation we had standing around the pile and intoning:

"It's fresh."

"It's green."

"It's bear shit."

And not the unforeseen struggle along the sketchy game trails, though calling them "trails" implies some sort of deliberate destination and purpose on the part of animals just trying to make an honest living. In the first nine hours we traveled just over four miles. Finally we sat on a river-smoothed driftwood log waving our hands over the maps and frowning at the GPS readings, and by noting the commonsense evidence of what our feet could testify, we produced this truth: there was no way to follow Wickersham's actual path along the pleasantly open ridges of the Kantishna Hills—not and arrive home by fall, much less in two weeks. Instead, the next morning, we became the Einsteins of the wilderness, trying to evade the space-time continuum by ditching the original route for a more direct but demanding route through the tangled forest and across the muskeg flats, enacting some painful equation of energy, mass, and speed, every bit of it relative.

How much I wanted this journey to proceed adventurously! Excitingly! But not too dangerously! And yet, if someone didn't die or escape death, what exactly was the point here? Once we'd abandoned Wickersham's route—on the very first day, embarrassingly enough—did it sound better or worse to acknowledge that this was far, far harder than I had ever imagined?

Along about the third day, mired in the wet, sucking muskeg with no trail to follow, consulting only fraying maps that said nothing more useful than *flat, green, white, river*, I realized this wasn't about reaching the mountain at all. I had embarked on this trip to find a story, to tell one, to make one. And the story wasn't about Wickersham or the mountain, but about me. At some point every expedition contracts, shrinking away from the grand verbs and minimizing the panorama, so that it inevitably, disappointingly, becomes all about you. Even my companions knew this was my story, not theirs. Hell, I'm not even naming them because there's no sense pretending to sort out their lives, their motives, their actions, when I can't even decipher my own.

I needed a narrative. The mountain so easily provides the key prop, a plaster lump of ice and granite rising to a glory measured precisely at 20,320 feet, a stage upon which people enact their own dramas of persistence and dedication and heroism in a literal embodiment of the story arc: the action rises, it climaxes, it descends. People climb up, they summit in triumph, they go back down. Unless they die, which instantly steepens the climax, makes it sharper and more meaningful. What plot did I have, now that Wickersham's journey was lost to me?

I didn't want to think about what would happen to this story if we traveled for two weeks to the foot of a mountain that couldn't be seen. I didn't know how to resolve that kind of blankness.

Still I scribbled away in a waterproof surveyor's notebook, recording snippets of conversation, lighting up when someone said something funny. I tried to describe stripping to bare skin to cross the coffee-black water of a deep slough, the way chill water crept up and floated the backpack, hunching me over and forcing out wheezing gasps that sounded like a bogged-down mule, the way mud grasped my shoes as I flailed and struggled to gain the shore. The way I panicked.

I searched for the proper words to convey the aching fear of crossing an ice bridge over Glacier Creek, but those that appeared didn't explain how our boots slid across that blue suspension, how my companion dragged the packs along the slick surface, and how I avoided looking into the roiling spring melt below. Instead another story emerged in my head as my feet crept forward—*cracking, shattering, sliding, falling, plunging, struggling, freezing, drowning*—all those horrible verbs that would mean we had miscalculated badly, that this sheen of late spring ice deceived. And when I leapt safely those last few steps to the mossy bank, I wasn't sure which story was the better one: the disaster unspooling in my mind, or the crossing that left us silly with relief on the other side.

I do know lost stories when I see them. They vibrated from the abandoned belongings of all who came before us, searching for gold or furs or peace, journeys that began in the twentieth century's earliest days. The trapper's cabin at the derelict trading post of Diamond was layered with the arcana of backwoods life: a forty-year-old Sno-Go rusting on its treads, an empty dogsled outfitted with canvas harnesses, a 1949 *Saturday Evening Post*, a board for stretching wolf pelts, unopened bags of Easter candy priced at thirty-nine cents. Wild rhubarb and grass pushed against the rotting logs. The tin roof and wood floor buckled and heaved in slow motion.

And that beautiful gold rush trail that appeared miraculously for a few miles, so that we strode, late in the day, through the forgotten settlement of Glacier City, the ruins flickering among groves of birch trees all of an age, cabins rotting into duff, and we walked past scattered middens of rusting tins and tarry barrels, ashes spilling from cast-iron stoves, wooden file drawers organizing fallen leaves from years past.

Time braided like the river here, spilling across floodplains, diverting into sloughs, disappearing below ground. None of this could properly be called wilderness. For ninety years homesteaders and trappers and prospectors have crossed and recrossed this landscape, looking for something, too. Long before them, the Athabascans named everything we saw. They moved through this country better than anybody, and the silence of their departure is the deepest silence of all.

The angled swoop of two marsh hawks disappearing into willow thickets. A pair of caribou that stare boldly before trotting away across the tundra. The nation-states of voles colonizing mossy slopes. The delicate shell of a caribou calf's hoof twisted into wolf scat. These reminded me of what persists, of what outlasts story every time.

It worried me, how Wickersham's journey was plenty more interesting and exciting than ours. His men shot at a bear, fought amongst themselves, dragged their mules along, hunted for caribou, capsized their raft in the rapids of the McKinley River, ate baked flour embedded with so many mosquitoes that they pretended it was currant bread.

How to convey the difficulty of this uneven terrain, the deep pleasure in moving no matter how labored each step becomes, the pride we took in solving problems like broken spectacles and a silt-clogged water filter? All of it paled before that one luminous moment when the sight of a junco nest embedded in the tundra raised me from the sodden misery of plodding across a ridge during a rainstorm.

I wanted a story shot through with humor, laced with poignancy. I hoped for an un-adventure story, one with no deaths or injuries, but with enough tension to make the reader wonder: *Will she get there? Is she strong enough? Will she return?*

But it was the story that separated me from what I was experiencing. I worried about how this journey was stringing itself along, what I'd tell others later when we returned (because of course we would return, wouldn't we?). I worried so much that only now and then could I glimpse what lay beyond. In the dimness of a midnight, as my companions burbled and sighed in sleep, I almost moaned aloud in fear and recognition as the world seeped into my flesh, as something inside dissolved, so that I felt scorched and blissful, not that those are the right words, not that I have the words at all.

I missed my husband terribly. I wasn't sure if I was walking to the mountain anymore, or if I was simply walking in place until one day I would magically find myself back in some forgettable life of daily dramas. Families must have been such a burden to explorers, whose minds could not help but reach homeward in the evenings once their feet had stopped moving. Wickersham never mentions his wife until the end of his chronicle. Mostly he natters on about losing the axe in a creek, or shooting fish in creeks, or taking down stories from the local Athabascans (who think his expedition is one of the silliest things they've ever heard of, because why would you climb that mountain, why wouldn't you just fall right off?).

Step by step, ache by ache, I tried to sense what those adventurers wanted most. Which kind of longing seemed most pure—the need to be part of something larger, to move outside the pale glow of safety and certainty? Or the yearning to be home, sheltered from the insistent world, from the blistering knowledge that anything can happen at any moment, for God's sake, you could die out here, why didn't you just stay home with your loved ones?

Mostly I tried not to think about the way the pack seemed to be wearing me as I walked, or the way the soggy earth tugged at my boots, a horrible refrain playing in my mind: *Sucking muck. Sucking muck.* Now that I had become a beast of my own burdens, I tried not to think of all those poor mules enlisted in past expeditions through Alaska: Mark and Hannah, Kid, Fannie, Beauty, General Jackson, General Weyler. Some stumbled through too many bogs and creeks and dropped, exhausted. Some were swept away by rivers. Some starved. The lucky ones were shot in the head and eaten.

Games played themselves in my head, the favorite being: walk all the way home from here, with nothing to show the way. Perhaps we could consult an internal lodestone, or sense our way along invisible meridians. Even a cat can find its owners across the country. Even a dog can retrace its steps. Even a bird can circumnavigate the globe. But we needed a mountain to guide us. A mountain we had yet to glimpse, which pissed me off the more I thought about it. We couldn't even see the damn thing from the Kantishna country because the land was rumpled and pleated and angled just enough to obscure it, despite its vaunted height. Even if it were within view, we might never lay eyes on it. It famously creates its own weather, concealing itself behind clouds so often in the summer that thousands of tourists go home unbelievers. What made me think that would not happen to us?

And so, in the dreaming half-dawn, I wondered if it was enough to hear the exact moment birds erupt into tangled songs, as if a conductor had swept a baton across the landscape. By fall they would be exhausted, singing twenty or more hours in the day. This happens every summer's day out here, I thought before falling asleep again. Every day, the world talks to itself, whether you are here or not.

During our rest day at Kantishna, when we ate in the road-house's elegant dining room, I remembered what was good about that half-remembered life of home—tomatoes, chairs, a roof. Ed and Gladys sat facing away from us and never said another word, prophetic or not. The next day, we walked down the road toward Wonder Lake until we could see the mountain for the first time, haloed against the blue sky, and thank heavens for that, because otherwise what kind of story would this be? But now, twenty-five miles away, the mountain wore a discouraging familiarity. It is the most famous face in Alaska, after all. Its image is flattened onto postcards and calendars, wrapped around candy bars, trapped inside snow globes, framed on canvas, pressed under glass. Most photographs capture it from this exact distance, reflected in the faithful mirror of Wonder Lake, dreamy and impossible.

I needed to be closer.

We walked.

Toward the end, the maps were useless. I smudged the topos with a penciled trail meant to suggest how far we had come, how far we must go, but it demonstrated only the narrowness of this passage, and how much lay beyond that trembling line that I would never see. Wickersham's hand-drawn chart—what a farce. Was this helix supposed to be a mountain ridge? Were those scribbles meant to describe a river? I closed one eye and held the copy against the landscape, against the modern maps, against what I knew to be true, and then I put them all away.

We walked.

Other stories should be resolved, but long ago I abandoned them. By now Wickersham is off arguing with fellow adventurer Webb, who packs up and leaves in disgust near the mountain's foot before returning, sullen and unhappy. The mules have run away again. That other fellow, McLeod, is afraid of mules almost as much as he fears bears, and Wickersham is deeply unsympathetic to this eccentricity. Despite their troubles, any day now their expedition will mount Peters Glacier, a thick blue tongue of ice that rises through the lesser peaks of Denali. They sincerely think they are bound for the summit in their foolish leather boots, with their alpenstocks and thick ropes.

All we wanted was to find Peters Glacier. Then we will stand at the foot of Denali, gaze upward, and go home.

My companions, what were they thinking? Now and then I spotted them at a distance, shouted greetings, met them to share meals and the tent. What they wanted, I still didn't know. I liked them, was grateful for their forbearance and trust, but probably I would never truly see them again after this time. Each of us made our own journey; each of us lived our own story.

What frightened me most about these last remaining miles was crossing the McKinley River, the way the water surged and muscled across the mile-wide gravel plain, rifting and splitting and grooving a score of waterways that ran opaque with gray glacial silt. There are rules for crossing rivers, but none of them addresses the cold that burns, the threatening sound of rocks tumbling and rolling beneath the surface, the hidden depths. One of my sandals tore free and floated downstream, but it was my companion who chased and rescued it from the current.

How easily I surrendered! We crossed, and crossed again, and again, knowing that soon enough we'd be crossing back.

This frightened me, too—that as we drew nearer, the mountain seemed farther away. We couldn't see it anymore. Clouds descended. The terrain obscured the horizon. Nothing to do, except keep walking toward a horizon that betrayed nothing.

One morning I searched the gear frantically for my spoon, because without it I'd be eating Cream of Wheat with a stick. But it was more than that. The one thing you could control out here was your own battered set of belongings. If a spoon could elude you, everything else might escape, too.

On the last day we would approach the mountain, we awoke to discover that of course the mountain was always there, clouds or not. It only seemed as if it had sailed up as we slept and moored itself to the horizon.

For days I had been walking toward an idea, a mark on the map, a phantom that materialized and evaporated at will. Now, here was this great shining hulk pinioning earth to sky. I tried to decide what I felt as we set out on these final few miles to the foot of Denali. Relief? Gladness? Fulfillment? Days ago on the Bearpaw River, when we were unsure we'd make it this far, one of my companions, the literary one, counseled *amor fate*: love your fate. Now I felt as if I had loved my fate, and fate had loved me in return.

The sun burned bold in a painfully blue sky, and the forest exhaled warm, peppery vapors of Labrador tea and dry moss and spruce needles. The riverbed narrowed as streams funneled into a single uncrossable channel. We passed islands of marooned vegetation, a bumbling porcupine trying to hide its head in a hole, and clear pools that made me long for soap and a washcloth.

The mountain loomed larger and yet somehow more unbelievable. At times it seemed composed of light and shadow, an airy confection excessive with parapets, towers, and buttresses. And sometimes it reared up among the reefs of surrounding peaks, frothy and windswept, a tsunami of snow that might topple at any moment. It was good we hadn't faced this mountain, this brilliant burning mass, every day. That might have been too much. Or it might have become too familiar.

For hours we walked through the cobbles. The river coursed through a deep gully, forcing us to climb gravel bluffs into the forest. Tiny avalanches cascaded from our feet. Peters Glacier had scraped through here on its retreat, studding the banks and the riverbed with boxcar-sized boulders. Only brush nubbed the slopes. We walked across the tracks of bears and wolves, searched the hills for watching eyes. Unseen climbers crawled somewhere on those white ridges above, trapped inside winter.

The day bunched behind us, and still no glacier. Soon we would have to turn back. The timelessness of the landscape was an illusion. These days of toil, the years of wondering, had narrowed to this point: we had less than an hour to walk before we must return to camp. My companions had jobs to return to, people who expected them, schedules to keep. I pretended I didn't, that I could spend as much time out here as I wanted. This lie was one more burden to carry, like a stone in my pack.

We hurried through mazes of boulders, trampling through gardens of wildflowers, until my companions paused on the crest of a small, mossy hill. Wasn't that Peters Glacier just ahead, that gritty inert stub? Nobody had to say this hillock was as far as our modest expedition would venture. We had walked forty-five miles, we had summited twelve feet, we had passed through days and nights of immeasurable length. We took the pictures, congratulated each other mildly. For years I had journeyed here, reading Wickersham's accounts, staring at maps, gazing at Denali from the ridge near my cabin. Yet never had I pictured this moment, balanced so delicately between arriving and departing, poised at the divide between where I have been and where I will go next.

For want of an hour, we had missed the glacier. The remaining distance—you could halve it, and halve it again and again, and never reach the other side. It was the flaw in the Persian carpet, the uneven stitch in the quilt, the rift that keeps the world from seamless perfection. It was the exact measure of longing.

If there was ever a moment to regret my original impulse, this was it. Ed and Gladys had spoken truly: *That's interesting, following in people's footsteps. You can never do that exactly, you know. You can never have their same thoughts. You can never know what it was like to be them at that time.*

Had I ever truly desired such a thing? I stood there, eyes fixed on a peak lofted at last from the two-dimensional photographs and the abstraction of maps. And still, how little anyone can ever know of such a mountain. I could walk toward it every day of my life and never be sure of understanding more than I did right then. Was this the small story I was making all this time? How foolish I felt, and yet at last it became clear that this narrative was just like my life, because it was my life—uncertain, unknowable, unfinished.

On our return, the mountain pressed behind, all that light and idea and density pushing against the back of my head. The hike to camp was long and tiring. I had seen the mountain, and yet my feet ached, and my skin burned, and my mouth thirsted. Many miles lay ahead; many river crossings awaited. Tomorrow I would turn a hundred times to gaze at those luminous slopes. Eventually one look would be the last.

Still to come was the time, late in the evening as the light bent over the horizon, when I would pause at the McKinley Bar and think seriously about returning to Peters Glacier alone, about fording that distance between what I'd hoped for and what I found. But this was a gap I feared I would never cross, no matter how far I traveled, no matter how closely I approached the mountain, no matter how many times and how many ways I tell this story. So I kept on, taking the long way home.

Fidelity

I SAW THE BEAR FIRST. I turned from the ocean's calm edge toward the dusky blue of Reid Glacier, and there it was, striding over the spit in the honeyed evening light, stiff green stalks of beach rye parting against its flanks. The bear was coming toward us. It was looking at us.

"There's a bear," I said. My voice was low. My husband was standing by the kayak and turned around to look. I did not know what else to say.

The bear kept coming. It was not so large as brown bears go, but it was large enough. Its amber pelt shaded into dark chocolate on its face and legs. Its head was low and its eyes small and intent, shining against the light. The bear was looking at us. To have a bear look at you and yet continue walking toward you means life is quite different from what you imagined.

"Hey bear," I called, raising my arms and waving. This is what you do at these times. Let the bear know you are there. Pretend to be larger than you are. Give the bear a chance to move away once it recognizes your presence. Speak in friendly but firm tones. "Hey bear, what's going on?" I said in a friendly way, and then I added firmly, "We don't want any trouble."

The bear did not pause. It walked deliberately in its pigeon-toed way across the cobbles, and now it was close enough that its intentions seemed to surge before it like a wave. Without meaning to, I stepped backward into the water. Cold seeped through my rubber boots. A person is not supposed to run away from bears. Anyway, there was nowhere to run, unless we skittered along the shore, crying out to the sky like sanderlings or oystercatchers.

Once that summer I went home to Fairbanks, after solstice, when the pendulum of the sun swings lower in the sky. Grass raged in the dim yard, and wild roses and fireweed pressed close to the cabin. I could not tell what my husband had been doing while I was away walking uninhabited shores, and floating rivers as wide as prairies, and sleeping beside unnamed mountains. One night in bed, thinking of all I'd been learning without him, I said, *You're a speed bump in my life.* It may have been the cruelest thing I've ever said. He looked at me and replied, *I love you with all of my heart. Why isn't that enough?* I couldn't say, but I knew the failure was in me, in wanting to make him something he was not and never would be.

Twenty feet away, the bear stopped and turned sideways, maybe to show us how big it was. It yawned. That glittering eye, sharp and knowing, did not leave us. Only a few times in your life are you asked to surrender completely to a moment. We could not have been more humble before this bear. Our hands were empty. The ocean was behind us. The bear was before us. Whatever happened next was entirely up to the bear.

It paced back and forth for a few minutes, clacking its teeth. We promised that we were just leaving, and when the tone of my voice edged into shrillness, it seemed to become more agitated. I calmed myself, reminded the bear that it was in charge. It shambled up the beach and nudged our gear, sniffed the food, and then kept walking until it reached the brush. It lofted itself onto its hind legs and beat at the alders with its paws, thrashing the leaves, and then it dropped to the ground and ripped at grass with its teeth. I had been afraid to look at its mouth, afraid to imagine it closing around my skull, tearing at my flesh. "You're beautiful," I said, in fear and gratitude, and I sang. I sang "Amazing Grace," just the first verse because that's all I know, and I sang it again louder as we crept around the beach and gathered our belongings so we could leave, so we could float on the water and watch the bear graze along the shoreline and for the first time notice the way it glowed in the fading sun.

I came to know my husband when he roomed with my high school sweetheart. Our courtship was accidental, secretive, conducted almost entirely by vibrations—albums played meaningfully late at night, e.e. cummings poems left at his bedroom door, the hesitant chords I fingered on the fine guitar he gave me. Only once did we discuss what to do next, by way of tossing a Frisbee back and forth in a meadow. I was seventeen, he was nineteen. We did not say we loved each other. We never kissed. I drank five rum and cherry Cokes and broke up with my boyfriend. Within two weeks we'd moved in together. Sometimes, in the nights that followed, the mattress tipped off the bed beneath us, and at breakfast our new roommate asked us if we ever slept. At our wedding five years later, in my parents' backyard on the Mendenhall River, he sang a song he had written for us. I kept my name, but still we liked to say the words: My husband. My wife.

He has always slept beautifully, easily, lashes dark against his clear skin, lips pressed together sweetly, black beard planing the smooth contours of his face. This distant peacefulness seemed like a rebuke, a way of refusing me, as I lay awake in the tent's faint light. Over and over I'd said, *Weren't we brave? Wasn't that amazing?* but I wanted him to notice how brave I'd been, how amazing I was, this new me who understood what to do, who did not panic or run away, who knew how to kayak and read charts and sing to bears. Now and then I lifted my head to peer along the beach. I was waiting. The only campsite we could find was a mile from the spit. And in the morning, as he dropped the tent and I stood at the tide line soaking in the water's bright calm, the bear walked out of the brush, looking at us once again, and I could not even feel surprised.

The bear followed him as he moved down the beach toward me, carrying a can of pepper spray. We stood side by side. Again the bear stopped yards away. Again it yawned and drooled and popped its jaws. I picked up a rock. Do bears remember people? After a few minutes, the bear turned up the beach. It walked across our tent, nosed the kayaks, and then stood and boxed some tree branches before falling to all fours and wandering back into the morning light.

I wasn't certain I wanted children. He knew he didn't. He convinced a doctor to give him a vasectomy when he was twenty-one, that's how sure he was. I went to college and he continued working in music stores. One day, a student in a microbiology class brought her newborn girl to school. She held the baby to her bare breast to soothe it, and something in me turned. I did not have the words to explain this feeling. Instead I told him the names of our children, after surgery or adoption or whatever. He nodded because he did not have the words to tell me no.

It's not necessary to talk about the drinking. Except to say we loved each other despite our silences. To say that now and then we talked about whether there was a problem, but sometimes I myself bought him fifths of excellent whiskey. To say how quiet it could be in our house, that golden bottle on the floor between us as he read within his pool of light, and I within mine.

Later you're afraid, when you think of all the things that can go wrong, when you understand how everything can change in a moment, just like that.

Mostly we thought of ourselves as happy, or at least not unhappy, but sometimes at night I rose from bed and slipped into my clothes and left. Nothing seemed to wake him. He could not sense my absence in his dreams. I drove for hours. I enjoyed weeping as I drove, searching for the saddest AM songs I could find. When I returned, he was always sleeping still. He would wake in the morning and never know I had gone.

Once, when I had been experiencing fainting spells, we sat in a neurologist's office as the doctor asked him about any weaknesses or lapses he might have noticed. *Does she ever get a blank look on her face, stare off into space?* the doctor wondered, pencil poised. We looked at each other and burst into laughter. He has spent so much of our marriage calling my name twice, searching for my eyeglasses and keys, quizzing me about where I might have left the car. As for me, I unzip what he has prematurely closed—his briefcases, his suitcases, even my bags and coats and wallets, all the things he cinches tight so nothing dangles or falls out.

The marriage counselor instructed us to list things we loved about each other, and things we didn't like, and things we'd never said before. She told me she had known plenty of mothers who wondered how happy their lives would be without children. Once she stifled a yawn as I talked. After a few weeks she said, *I don't usually tell people things like this, but I have a good feeling about you two. I think you'll make it.* For years, I thought about her comment the way I read my horoscope each morning: hopefully, doubtfully.

We paddled hard away from the beach, away from that bear. In the bow I turned my head so he could hear me. I wanted to talk about what might have happened if I had been sitting with my back to the bear when it had appeared over the spit, if we had still been in our tent when it emerged from the brush. "It didn't happen that way," he said. "It doesn't matter." He doesn't like imagining the worst. At camp, on the gray silt of a glacial outwash, we ate dinner with our backs to the water, scanning the rocky slopes for movement. We did not speak. Growlers and bergy bits rolled in the fjord, and calving ice echoed against the granite cliffs. Cold radiated from the water, the ground, the shadows. There were no trees or brush, so we built a fire from Presto logs we'd wedged into the kayak bow. That basin was a hard place to be, rasped bare by receding ice. There was no place to camp where bears would not be. We knew that before we came.

Married friends divorced. Unmarried friends split up. Reconciliation is what we claimed, over and over, for those twenty-three years gone by. And how proud we were of this, how much we'd relinquished for each other, how much we'd surrendered. After he quit drinking, he took my hands one day and said that if I wanted children, we would somehow make them or find them, and that's when I could let go of those shadowy babies and look elsewhere for what could bind me to this world. When I asked him to make this trip to Glacier Bay with me, to do this one thing for me, he could not say, *No, thanks,* and I could not say, *Never mind, this isn't what I'm asking for anyway.*

We fought. Probably I started it. I huddled on a stone by the fire and wept and shouted, and he stood on the other side of the artificial flames and looked at me with fury and bewilderment. We said all the things people say when they have slept together naked every night and awakened together every morning knowing what they know, having forgiven each other over and over and still able to find more that needs forgiving. *You always. You never. Why can't you? Why didn't you?* They scraped us clean, those words, stripped us into weary silence.

Whenever I thought of leaving, I'd remember a winter afternoon when he leaned over the chair in which I sat reading and circled me with his arms. I dropped my book and looked at our hands, mine cupped within his. *I love you,* he whispered against the back of my neck, and as he spoke, a blue-green vein in my wrist pulsed with all that hot blood moving just beneath the surface, that faithful tide sweeping toward my heart each moment.

Now we knew all the possibilities, and still we could not have expected to stoop from the tent the third morning and see two young brown bears shuffling along the tide line toward us. Part of me wanted to remain silent and see if the bears would pass by. But we moved up the slope and out of their path, and when they drew near we called, "Hey bears! Do you see us? Here we are!" They rose to their hind legs and peered at us before they dropped and began loping uphill, rumps jogging, glancing over their shoulders now and then as they moved among the boulders. "About time a fucking bear ran away," he muttered.

I felt kindly toward those bears. They had reestablished my faith in what bears are and what we are, and how we all should believe in the plain truth of each other.

In that moment like no other moment between us, I look away from his dark and knowing eyes. It's too much, what's he giving me, all those good and painful years behind us, all those years of love and loss to come.

That night and the next we slept without a tent on a rocky knoll. The tide slipped through the gulch, splitting the knobby fist from the mainland and islanding us. We could not see the glacier just beyond, but chill gusts and the crack of avalanching ice swept over us. We built a fire on platters of shale and watched seals swim in the quivering sea below. The sky thinned into indigo. High above, gulls floated with wing tips grazing stars.

Such a relief to be still and quiet, to lie there open to the world and returned to ourselves. I slept with a hand tucked into his sleeping bag, one palm pressed against that steady warmth. In the morning, we sat and watched the clear light fill the stony basin, grateful that for once there was nothing more to say.

Sometimes we talk about that raw place, quartered by stone, ocean, sky, and ice, where every creature must remain true to its own essential nature to survive. Once I told him that for a frightening time, I did not love him. *I've never stopped loving you*, is all he said. Perhaps I had forgotten what endures. Ice cracks, but glaciers flow onward. The earth trembles, but mountains stand. Tides rise and tides fall, but the ocean persists. Fidelity is what saved us, I suppose. Most likely fidelity will rescue us again.

That bear still walks those shores, you know. It refuses to surrender even a slim margin of territory. Of course, it does not know how to be anything but itself, its bold and willful self. I think sometimes about that dark shape as it approaches, about its level and knowing look, and I think how all we can do is yield to its awful beauty and say, *Hey bear. I see you, too.*

The Mapmaker

SGT. WILLIAM YANERT RECEIVES ORDERS to strike north toward the Tanana River, and so he does. He is in for a thrashing from a pitiless terrain, and he knows it. It is mid-August, and with every day that passes, winter draws near. Three rivers tangle around him—the Susitna, the Talkeetna, the Chulitna—each with its own notion of how best to navigate this disorderly landscape. Yanert won't force his way along. He knows Alaska is country you must ease your way through. It's you who needs the pushing.

The officers in charge of this summer's military explorations seem to make things up as they go, so their vague orders do not surprise Yanert. This is what the army does in Alaska in 1898: It explores. It describes. It surveys. It dispatches men to cut trails, and map routes to the Yukon River and the goldfields of Interior Alaska, and report on the conditions of the Natives. Sometimes the Natives save these men, who starve and weaken due to the difficulties of cutting trails and mapping routes in a country that is provident in space and often empty of food.

Yanert stands just over five foot five, and he has brown hair and blue eyes. He is thirty-five, and as age whitens his hair and beard, people will say he is the reincarnation of Buffalo Bill Cody. He was born in Prussia, but since he was a teenager he has served as a U.S. Cavalry soldier. During the Klondike gold mania, the army sent him north to Skagway, where he walked the Dyea Trail to report on the argonauts' progress. Now as a soldier in Capt. E. F. Glenn's exploring expedition, he is the physical extension—the squinting eyes, strong legs, and tender, bleeding feet—of the army's interest in Alaska.

Accompanying Yanert is Private Jones of Company D and an Indian guide named Bate. The men carry seventy pounds of gear apiece. During the next thirty-two days, Yanert washes down a stream and nearly through a canyon. He loses a shoe in a bad crossing, and so he slices up his half of a tent for footwear and walks until the canvas shreds away. Lacking any shelter, he sleeps in the open. The men run out of provisions and eat game and berries. The guide quits, but Yanert continues until he reaches the Nenana River and the chilling nights tell him it is time to return to his detachment, which he does, by foot and by raft.

He maps what he sees and makes his official report in bland prose, mentioning none of his difficulties save for a passing reference to traveling barefoot. Yanert's reports reveal little of the man who will become known throughout the north for his hand-colored cartoons and practical jokes, the man who will be memorialized by newspapers as the "Sage of the Yukon" and "Mysterious Yanert," because, one writer notes, it is a mystery "why so pleasing a personality and one possessing unusual mental traits and social qualities should place himself out of touch with his own kind."

But now, in the middle of his life, he is a man who can find his way anywhere, a man who can walk in bare feet on cold ground through unmapped territory, a man looking for a place to make his home at last.

My husband and I moved to Anchorage a few years ago. Never did I think I would exchange Fairbanks for a city so outsized and overstimulating. So much would be left behind: The slope where three red foxes trotted out of tall grass and glanced at me before disappearing. The creaking of hundreds of sandhill cranes spiraling together in a fall-blued sky, kettling up before turning south. The heat and light of birch logs firing in a winter sauna. The clear ice of the upper Chena River fractured into galaxies and nebulae inches below the surface. What I called home was mostly an atlas of experiences hoarded from the landscape. But always, for me, restlessness minnows through the blood.

On our last day in Fairbanks, I dug up my delphiniums and irises and blue poppies, splitting root-balls and making cuttings to distribute to friends. I packed rocks and shells and animal skulls gathered from the Beaufort Sea, the Salcha River, the Canadian Tombstones, the Copper River. I wrapped bones and antlers and feathers from Wickersham Dome, Johns Hopkins Inlet, Peters Glacier, Dutch Harbor, the Fortymile country, Lituya Bay.

I found the blue-eyed cat, dazed by the tranquilizers I'd fed her, creeping among wild roses blooming at the yard's edge. She had been running away an inch at a time all day. My husband climbed into a rental van tilting with all that could not be abandoned. I piled the two dogs and the limp cat into the car, and as we lurched up the driveway, I said good-bye to the other cat, the dead one still in her little wooden box deep in the yard.

Going south, we crossed the rivers Chena, Nenana, Tanana, Chulitna, Susitna, Matanuska, and Knik, until we reached our new house at Peters Creek. There I burrowed plants into the June-warmed earth, and scattered rocks and bones about, and every evening looked north across Knik Arm at the light purpling the horizon.

In 1903 Yanert, no longer the army's man, snowshoes across the flats at fifty below until he stops at a northern bend of the Yukon River, twenty miles south of the Arctic Circle and a few miles below the mouth of the Hodzana River. It's a mystery how he knows this is the place, rather than the mountainous landscape he traversed in what we know today as Broad Pass, or the hills around Eagle, where he worked as a scout.

He lives in a tent until he finishes building a cabin and a cache. He names the place Purgatory because, he writes to friends, "to most people it is such a Hell of a place to live." Two years later his brother Herman arrives.

What is there to do in Purgatory? Why, live, of course. Bill Yanert believes this is the land of his desire. He and Herman hunt and trap, cut wood, tramp around. In the summers, they grow vegetables and welcome rare travelers, even the annoying ones, even the visitor who brings the surprising news that Christ has risen. Herman is the cook; they joke that Bill is the gentleman artist. From antler, wood, and bone, he carves figures of animals, miners, Natives, and scenes from Hamlet and Macbeth translated to a northern setting. He reads Dante and other classics, and he writes doggerel. He illustrates his poems with cartoons of wildlife, dogs, and himself, adding such titles as "The Perplexed Woodsman" or "The Old Dog's Dream." Eventually the cabin walls are so thick with paintings and drawings that the logs are barely visible.

"I think there is more joy to be had out of what one does with brush or pen or tools, than out of the things we are driven to do by our everlasting need of bread and butter," he writes.

He has not forgotten the skills that brought him into the country. In 1916, he makes an exquisite chart that today can be held against official maps and matched lake by lake, hill by hill. It is a portrait of perhaps thirty by thirty-five miles of the landscape surrounding Purgatory. He titles it "A Fraction of the Yukon Flats."

The Yukon River unravels across the paper like fraying rope. He marks the village of Beaver, a cabin that belongs to someone named Oury, an abandoned mail camp. A few trails skitter across the paper in dots that look like vole tracks. He names names, and because he does not know the Athabascan words for this territory, most of them are plain: Duck Creek, Bear Lake, Birch Lake, Beaver Slough. Later Yanert will complain to his friend Margaret (Mardy) Murie about the uninspiring quality of these northern names: Willow, Alder, Moose, Swede, Fourth of July, Last Chance.

"These seem the only names Alaskans can think of, there isn't a sign of romance, poetry, and such in the prospector's nomenclature!—Think of 'Cripple Creek'—I could flatten a man's nose for that! Every creek, to my mind, is a streak of beauty; it adorns a mountainside as does a whisp of hair a girl's face."

He thinks sometimes of girls he might have married, girls he might have fathered. In thanking Mardy for a photograph of her daughter, Joanne, he muses: "I see her smiling right in my face, and I can't help thinking that had so lovely a girl smiled at me in the long-ago, I never would have developed into the single-harness ass I have been all my life!"

But that comes later. Now, deep into his life, he draws his *mappae mundi*, and on it he records what he knows of his world, just a fraction, as he notes, but a fraction that encompasses a thousand square miles. He is witness and scribe to the cranks and turns of the fickle Yukon River, to the deceptively porous quality of the earth, to the exuberance of vegetation that hinders summer travel. He draws his life.

In ornate script, he explains what extends beyond the paper. *This ridge continues westward* and *Lost Creek has its source in the Mountains to the South; they adjoin those of Hess Creek,* and so on. He tells what he knows and does not claim more than he should. *The entire area of low ground is a jungle covered bog liable to inundation by the Yukon.* And: *All water flowing from this ridge is lost in the swamp at its foot.* He is the Ptolemy of Purgatory, describing what is known of the earth's surface in his time, his place. The name of his home is a tiny fish floating in the river.

Could you draw your fraction, hill by creek by lake? Could you map even the smallest part of your territory? And would your home be the largest or smallest thing on your map?

People ask how I like Anchorage, and I say, cagily, "I like it more than I thought I would." This is true. The pleasures of the city—food, music, the ease of commerce—fade quickly, but unexpected rewards appear. The Chugach Mountains save me from despair at least once a day. When traffic mires me, or work maddens me, I lift my eyes to the cut and swoop of those peaks, and it is calming. Our first summer we walked some of the ridges and valleys, finding it a strange comfort during one hike to come upon two distant brown bears gnawing on a moose, their faces bloody and satisfied. Every morning I look for Denali, as if it were a compass. But usually I tell my questioners, so there is no mistaking my intentions, so there is no question of falling in love with this place, that we are only pausing here, that we are on our way to somewhere else.

One Christmas, Bill and Herman carve a wooden devil head. This becomes Old Saint Nick, the patron saint of Purgatory. They drape the effigy in red calico, with moose antlers for horns and bottle glass for eyes. That is what living alone year after year can do to you. They erect the puppet on the river-bank, and when steamboats pass, they dash out and yank ropes so that the devil waves a handkerchief at startled passengers.

Later they add a bearskin-covered imp that pops from the ground. The boats begin stopping and disgorging tourists, and Bill sells them "Yukon Breezes," a hand-colored book of his poems and cartoons, for five dollars each. He becomes famous, in a northerly way.

In 1931, Bill begins traveling free on the steamer *Yukon* because he entertains the passengers so well. "I made four trips just to dish up a lot of Alaska guff to the tourists who come up here every summer," he writes. "Gee, how I did stuff them! . . . Gosh what a nice thing it is to be able to load those folks with yarns of the wilds! They swallow almost anything like a hungry trout!"

He likes exclamation points. That's the kind of man he is, exclaiming about the odd turns and notions that will come to a person, out there on the Yukon. Above the Yanerts' cabin door a carved sign reads, "Where the world's mad clamor is gagged and fettered and laughed to scorn by solitude." Every time Bill reads of some new foolishness in the civilized world, he reminds his correspondents why he sticks to Purgatory: "It is just because of the ways of you city folks that I took to the woods long ago where I can take a drink out of my old hat any time without having to pay for it."

The truth is, he is the kind of hermit who likes talking. The nearest neighbor to Bill and Herman lives twenty-three miles away. "He came up just to see were we alive yet, and to show us that he is. But, Gee, how we did talk after not talking all those months since September!" It was June.

Distances do not bother Bill. He was born to collapse distance, one step at a time. In January of 1940, when he is seventy-six years old, he snowshoes to Beaver, forty-five miles by river but abbreviated some by a trail he cut in the fall. He wants to mail some letters he has labored over. The journey takes him eight and a half hours. It is a trip he repeats three times in one winter.

Winter is his season, anyway. "Summer with us is a time-killing proposition at best; about the sole thing we can do, is lug in the poles for the Winter's firing." Summer is heat and mosquitoes and the near-impossibility of travel, unless by boat. But winter is slow and deep, a thickness laid across the land. Sometimes, standing with his boots squeaking against the dry snow, he hears the northern lights, and when he writes the Geological Survey to say so, scientists there write back and ask him to tell them more. "None of the scientists have ever had a chance to hear the noise as none of them have lived in the Far North any length of time," he notes.

Herman and Bill rhyme and carve and listen their way through winter. How still it must have seemed in 1928–29, when Herman went downriver to Stevens Village. Bill writes: "I have spent a lonesome winter; the only evidence of others rummaging around in the Universe, that come to my notice, were some shots fired up-river on Nov. 18th, then an Airplane whirred westward directly overhead. On Dec. 23, it was 30 below 0 at the time and perhaps it was Santa Claus. I wonder what he thought of the little black animal he saw beneath him crossing a lake!"

Later he learns that a man named Arnold, who was staying at a deserted cabin seven miles away to cut wood for summer's steamboats, has been found dead by a trapper, "froze stiffer'n a poker in the cabin." Bill paid no attention to the shots that must have been fired by Arnold. They were too irregular, he explains, as if someone had been shooting at moose or some running animal, not signaling for help. "Well, a lot of us who live off in the woods are fated to that sort of cashing in; strange the old man did not know how to fire a signal——."

Bill thinks he is not sentimental about such things. A few years later he hears of a trapper who shot himself near Fort Yukon rather than freeze to death in a blizzard. He writes to Mardy: "I warned him once not to go off by himself any longer as he had had a slight stroke of paralysis; he said then: 'Oh, I've got a gun in the boat that is just the right length to put my toe on the trigger and let her go!'—Nothing like sticking to one's convictions, is there?"

One day a few years ago, I was wandering down a dirt track in Gustavus, a place where maybe four hundred people live scattered among the spruce trees and fields along Icy Strait, near Glacier Bay. A house's blue roof mushroomed from a tidal meadow awash in lupine, fireweed, and sharp, gleaming grass as high as your waist. A stream lazed through the meadow, and by the road someone had groomed a small vegetable plot, the most orderly thing in sight. A For Sale sign was nailed to the house.

For an idle morning or so, I imagined living there, though I had no money or reason to buy this house. We lived in a little log cabin in Fairbanks surrounded by aspen and birch trees. We owned beachfront property on an island near Petersburg. I had been hedging my bets, not quite sure where I'd settle.

Of course it was neither the house in Gustavus that I wanted, nor simply another bit of land. I wanted the south wind from Icy Strait, and the capillary draw of the briny stream, the sleep that comes with slow rain, and the dependability of purple iris hazing the meadow each and every spring.

When I next visited Gustavus, the little house was still for sale. No good comes from ignoring omens. I photographed it from the road and sent the film to my husband with instructions to develop the photographs, fall in love, and then visit the bank and ask for money. Perhaps we would not live in this place just yet, but nevertheless this was to be our home, so it would be best to buy it now, while it was for sale. He finally agreed, solving for X in one of those marital quadratic equations: He loves me, and I love the house, and though he does not love the house yet, some day he will.

Even in his hermit's eddy, there on the Yukon River, Bill Yanert knows the world changes around him. One day in October 1931 Herman Yanert hears a strange hum and calls for his brother. He thinks an earthquake must be coming. An airplane swoops overhead. It is the mail plane, and its passage is erasing the dogsled postal service, a system that furrows winter with valuable trails all through the north.

"Do you know that Alaska has undergone an enormous change since you were here?" Bill reminds Mardy after a rare visit to Fairbanks. "New faces everywhere and civilization's unlovely innovations are crowding the ways of old out of existence. I do not like Alaska's new face a bit!"

In 1940, Bill rides his first airplane while returning from Seattle, where he has undergone an operation at what he calls the "emporium of slashed vitals." His back has been bothering him.

The Fairbanks doctor diagnoses arthritis of the spine, but what Bill knows is he cannot sleep through the night.

Though he refuses to ride in automobiles, he is not in the least afraid of airplanes and the possibility of crashing. "This was because I knew that in such a case, I would land on the rocky crust of this globe so hard that I would be wrecked entirely and painlessly, which would hardly be the case in an Auto collision. It isn't the fear of outright death that makes me 'leery' about Auto riding, no, the thought of winding up crippled for life is what buffaloes me. How deep-rooted that dread is in me."

Think, then, of the old man in a dim ward late in 1941, scribbling to Mardy Murie in pencil and apologizing for his uneven lines. He is in a slow-motion wreck, marooned in the veterans' hospital in Portland where he will spend the last four months of his life. A kindly woman, the wife of his neighbor in the ward, makes him comfortable in his bed. He has no one else. Doctors don't know what to tell him, but the paralysis that has seized his muscles frightens him.

He hears that his old friend the riverboat *Yukon* has struck a rock. Perhaps that is why he writes:

> *They say a drowning man sees his life reeled off in his last moments. Never having gone under for the last time I cannot say is it time, but Mardy, since lying half here day after day the minutest details of my life have come to mind while I am wondering at myself and what all this may mean. Am I actually sinking out of sight?*

One spring I spent a few days trying to be quiet in a tiny cabin on Resurrection Bay. The window overlooked the long silver inlet, and spiders dangled outside the panes. The light faded in the same radiant way that stained glass dims a chapel. I didn't know this place at all, yet how much seemed familiar. In the morning the ocean presented the same clean, dense, and promising smells I grew up with in Juneau. I recognized, too, the lumpy mountains I couldn't name; the eagle rasping like an ungreased hinge, opening and closing, opening and closing; the occasional mad rush of waves against the shore. And I strained to hear these things, because beside the cabin stretched a long row of white RVs, lined up against the rocky shore like piglets. Through the cabin's thin walls I heard engines, conversations, dogs, and children, and I clapped headphones to my ears and listened to Sarah Vaughan instead of to the sea of people.

One evening, after everybody had shuttered themselves within their tin can homes, I saw from the window a ripple, a flipping, in the dark water. I walked to the tide's edge to watch two sea otters rassling like puppies, leaping like kittens, looping the loop through the sea. What I longed to see lay just beneath the surface, where they swam against a liquid sky. This must mean home to a sea otter—the constant motion between the unknown and the familiar, the flickering border between what we have and what we want.

Growing older by the Yukon River, Bill Yanert sometimes thought of death, once even composing a poem called "The Dying Yukoner," in which he asks to be buried in the Yukon

Flats with his rifle and a score of rounds and a compass, items he figures he will need in heaven. He concluded:

> *Dig me a grave on some timbered hill*
> *Where the winds rove wild and free,*
> *Blaze there a spruce, mark it: OLD BILL,*
> *Mush off and let me be!*

And he added a postscript: *Mean every word of it, too!*

In the veterans' hospital in Portland, he asks that his heart be cut out and buried at Purgatory. He knows he will never see his home again. But the hospital is perhaps not able to understand such requests, or to abide by them, and so after he dies they cremate him and ship his ashes to Beaver. Herman Yanert learns his brother is dead when he picks up his mail.

Who knows why Herman obscures the placement of his brother's remains? He writes to Mardy: "Have buried Bill's ashes in the place designated by him. The grave is _____ on a _____ N.W. of this cabin at Purgatory and is well secluded from view. Here he will wait for eternity."

No one will go to Purgatory with me. It wouldn't be hard to find. Modern maps show it in letters much bolder than those used by Bill on his map. Canoeing downriver from the village of Beaver would be easiest, but I am a wretched paddler, and my friends are not so interested in a homestead abandoned sixty years ago, if any of it even remains. To them, the maps show a flat and leaky landscape, potholed with lakes and sloughs and oxbows shaped like protozoans. The very words "Yukon Flats"

might as well declare "mosquitoes by the millions." That much the maps can tell you, if you know how to read them.

I thought I might wander around the homestead, unfold a copy of his hand-drawn map, and use my feet to trace its contours and knowledge, to match what was in his head and heart against what he charted. Because who did William Yanert draw his map for, if not someone like me?

Once, when oral historians were interviewing Susie Williams, a Koyukon Athabascan elder, about a particular place on the Koyukuk River, she said she didn't know it.

"But we know you camped here," an interviewer said.

"Yes," Williams said, "but I don't know the stories that belong to that place."

What could Purgatory tell me that I don't already know? That a professional wanderer finally came to know this one piece of land so well that he could tell a little story about it with his map, that the northern lights sang to him, that he loved solitude and winter? None of this spared the old mapmaker from dying far from the one place he longed to be.

A year after we moved to Anchorage we climbed Bear Mountain behind our house. All winter I had imagined scrambling onto the summit's plateau. I didn't want to use a trail, having in mind some foolishness about "discovering" my way up the mountain. But when my husband and I stood among the greening birches, all sight of our destination obscured by tangled underbrush, I realized I was no Bill Yanert. So we skirted the mountain's foot and hiked a root-bound path through the forest. The trail shot through a gully running with snowmelt, and we scrambled hand over hand along the last steep ridge, faces hovering above last year's berries and this year's buds.

The ghostly green of reindeer lichens powdered beneath our feet as we drifted toward the mountain's edge. Bearberries snuggled against the tundra in dull black clusters, and when we rested, shriveled cranberries stained our legs and rear ends. A marsh hawk tilted at the rim and dropped from sight.

Behind us the bare Chugach Mountains crested like waves. To the northeast the Talkeetna Mountains folded and refolded themselves before flattening into the lowlands. The Alaska Range rose against the horizon. From our vantage of three thousand feet, we could see how the Knik River creases the mudflats on its way to Cook Inlet, and how the flood tide covers the river's passage. Hidden among the trees is the village of Idluytnu—Eklutna is what the maps say—where Dena'ina Athabascans settled long before the Russians or Captain Cook snooped around.

Many military explorers began their inland journeys here. Yanert himself took charge of the army's camp at Knik during the winter of 1898–99. I liked thinking that he and I had each spent a winter beside the same river. But of course it's not the same river at all, not for Yanert, not for the Dena'ina, not for me. *Other waters are ever flowing on to you,* said Heraclitus.

But Yanert would recognize still the scent of new leaves syruping the air. The slow unfisting of fiddleheads. Songs of identity and desire sifting down from robins and sparrows and chickadees. Afternoon clouds rucking over the mountains. And wouldn't he know the shine that comes from leaves shivery in the wind, from the sheen of rain, from every slip of water spangling beneath the sky?

Almost every morning I study a picture of the house we haven't yet slept in. It occurs to me I am escaping to Gustavus an inch at a time, just as my doped-up cat made her slow-motion break for the woods when we left Fairbanks. When I hold that photograph, I imagine how Scott and I will drape the garden with seaweed. We'll be glad of neighbors and gladder still of solitude. We'll drink rainwater gathered in the cistern and soak in the wood-fired horse trough tucked among the spruce. Some afternoons we will lie in beach rye and iris, the rushes fragrant from our crushing, and above us creamy Queen Anne's lace will quiver. Below us the earth, relieved from the weight of glaciers, will swell at the dizzying rate of one inch per year, and we'll measure our life in fractions reclaimed. We do not find our homes. We map them inch by inch, story by story, day by day.

Hypothetical Geographies

How do you find your way there? More importantly, will you ever find your way back? Tucked into a newspaper article about a widow's relentless search for her husband's missing plane appears this astonishing fact: Alaska State Troopers know of 711 people missing somewhere in the wilderness as of August 2006. It's easy to say they vanished or they disappeared, but of course they didn't. They simply no longer remain within our sight. Let us assume that most of them did not choose this.

A hundred times I've fiddled with my compass, practicing how to triangulate my position so I can mark it on a map, or adjusting the declination to account for a magnetic pole that even now migrates toward Siberia. This is book learning, nothing that comes naturally. And how entrancing it is to stand outside aiming my GPS at the sky as phantom satellites reassure me from outer space: "You are here . . . you are here . . . you are here." But sometimes fog rolls in and the compass gestures toward blankness, GPS batteries run low, or satellites evaporate beyond the horizon. Sometimes the instruments proclaim a precise longitude and latitude, sometimes they can tell me exactly where I've been and how far I'll need to go, yet still I'll look around and the hills remain mute, with nothing at all to say.

The all-purpose term for how people move through the world is deceptively simple: *wayfinding*. Today we discuss wayfinding as methods of designing signs or organizing structures or creating a "grammar of movement" (whatever that is) to help us navigate efficiently through "built environments," such as city streets, or plazas, or the virtual worlds of cyberspace. But the history of humans is really the history of navigating through an unknown, perilous world, so that those who venture out of sight may one day return to tell what they found.

Once there were a hundred methods of wayfinding. It's said that westering Vikings tossed ravens into the air to determine which direction to sail, though surely ravens were an unusually truculent device. Travelers journeying beyond visible landmarks used dead reckoning to mark their progress by calculating their speed and direction from a fixed position—the home port, or the last oasis, or wherever they slept last night. People like Christopher Columbus sailed off the map and back onto it again using nothing more complicated than a stick and knotted rope to measure speed and a compass to set the course. Much of the world was explored and mapped by heeding the movements of the sun, the moon, and the stars. Celestial navigation has proved so dependable that Apollo lunar astronauts relied on thirty-seven stars to guide their passages.

The instruments of wayfinding have grown ever more elaborate over the centuries as the world has sharpened into focus. Hourglasses have evolved into chronometers. The thickness of fingers held against a horizon has become the delicate mechanism of astrolabes and sextants. Clay tablets etched with crude maps have multiplied into geographic information systems. And still we look toward heaven, where the fixed stares of geosynchronous satellites calculate everything we need to know, including what our houses look like from twenty-two thousand miles above the earth's surface.

The finest instrument of orientation is the one we rarely consult anymore: the human mind, housed in the fragile casing of a body, exquisitely tuned to divine the texture of snow, the direction of wind, the temperament of the sea. It can help you find your way across a landscape as complicated and expansive as Alaska or yourself. But remember that before the locomotive, the plane, the automobile, the computer, we moved differently through time and space, that at one time natural meant, as writer Rebecca Solnit explains, "not where you were, but how you moved through it."

One summer, in the Canadian town of Inuvik on the Mackenzie River Delta, I bought a small soapstone figure carved to represent slabs of rock stacked into a vaguely human shape. The sculpture was the white-flecked green of a winter ocean, small enough to fill the hand with a satisfying heft. A twelve-year-old Inuit girl chiseled and polished it into shape as I watched, just as her father taught her, and then she sold it to me in her first transaction as a carver. For a long time I called the figure an *inuksuk* because so many others do. The oddly compelling shape has lodged itself in popular imagination, appearing on the flag of the newest Canadian province, Nunuvut, and as an award in the Ford Motor Company that "embodies the essence of what it takes to excel in the marketplace."

Canadian writer Norman Hallendy explains that this icon is actually an *innunguaq*, meaning "in the likeness of a human." The true *inuksuit*, the plural of *inuksuk*, are cairnlike arrangements of stone and sometimes bone and wood, "that which acts in the capacity of a human." They are meant to convey specific meanings to Inuit travelers. For decades Hallendy traveled with elders on Baffin Island to photograph examples of *inuksuit* erected throughout the arctic landscape. His mentors explained that *inuksuit* offer important meanings to hunters and other travelers, and Hallendy describes them as the navigational equivalent of modern maps and satellite photos. Some are "deconfusers," a kind of stone memo that might, for example, remind a hunter where he stored his tools. Others are pointers, perhaps as simple as a triangular rock aimed toward a significant shoreline. Stone platters assembled into tall pyramids or wedges might mark headlands or hunting sites, while others balanced into frames provide sight lines, so a traveler could look through one window to locate the next figure or note an important celestial alignment. They suggest routes home, signal shifts in the landscape, or mark places of spiritual significance, of justice, of power. Some create private messages. Their original meaning depends on your ability to apprehend the maker's intention.

Like any other instrument, without someone to teach you how to use it, an *inuksuk* speaks to no one but itself. Just as important is your own awareness of the landscape. Hallendy once visited a shaman initiation site where the stone figure marked a moment of great enlightenment. The peaceful landscape revealed nothing of the power that had once infused it until he happened to sit beside the marker. He wrote:

> *Now, the* Angaku'qarvik *loomed over me. I could feel the warmth of the earth and hear what I believed was the wind make strange sounds as it moved through the crevices of the stone figure. I struggled to keep observation apart from imagination. Still, a sense of awe overcame me as I watched a million crystalline surfaces form on the stones of the* Angaku'qarvik *like a sky full of stars on a clear winter night. A sense of foreboding entered me. After a time I left, careful not to touch the object for I now understood to do so would certainly invite misfortune.*

Stone messengers stand mute throughout the north. Several hundred rock cairns radiate in lines around Agiak Lake in Alaska's Brooks Range, arranged to help hunters drive caribou toward their spear points, but most stone sentinels on ridges or beside rivers represent the simplest message of all: *I was here.* Cairns erected with more subtle codes have eroded into silence, now that wayfarers have disappeared. One young villager intrigued by Unalakleet's slate monuments asked elders what they knew; one man thought perhaps they'd marked tribal lands long ago, and a woman said she'd once been told that passing travelers added stones "just to let people know they've been there."

I wish I'd asked someone in Toksook Bay about the large cairn on the mound behind the village. A wind scouring the snow discouraged me from setting out to have a closer look. That afternoon, as I waited around the high school where all visitors to the Nelson Island village stay, a Yup'ik man leaned against the main entrance and studied the weather outside. He said conversationally that probably things would calm down later (and he was right). He'd grown up learning to read the weather by listening to his grandfather. Hunters couldn't afford not to understand how wind and snow and clouds and temperatures worked, he said. "I'm a human barometer," he added, grinning suddenly.

And more, no doubt. There's a Web site titled Yup'ik Tundra Navigation that explains how a sixty-five-year-old Akiachak elder named Fred George navigates ninety miles to his winter fish camp on the Yukon River at night. The researcher, Claudette Englom Bradley, used pipe cleaners to form constellations on the inside of a black umbrella so she could understand how Fred George calculates his position by the stars, measuring the position of *Tunturyuk* (the Big Dipper) by using his watch and his hand.

By traveling with George one March, Bradley also learned how the elder senses the proper course through the effects of wind and snow on the landscape. Prevailing northeasters carve snow into patterns of frozen waves on lake surfaces, so if George is headed in the proper direction he feels a certain rhythmic surge of the snowmachine through his body. If the rhythm changes, he knows he is off course. (It comes as no surprise that he recognizes each lake between the Kuskokwim and the Yukon rivers—and there are scores—by their Yup'ik names.) While traveling across tundra, he notes the south-westerly lean of the sparse trees and of frozen grass. He also checks his positions by landmarks—streams, cabins, distant mountains. When Venus (known to Akiachak villagers as *Unuakum Agyartaa*) takes its place as the morning star, it leads him home. The entire landscape functions as a compass—or rather, he does.

These wayfinding techniques echo those of the great Polynesian navigators, who crossed open ocean without using sextants, compasses, or any such devices. Nainoa Thompson is the first modern Polynesian to learn the science of wayfinding. In a Public Broadcasting Service documentary, he described learning to identify more than two hundred stars, memorizing their positions, and reading the movements of waves, the angle of the sun, the behavior of birds. Even a cloudy sky doesn't interfere with master voyagers. Thompson's mentor, a Micronesian named Mau Piailug, learned as a child from his grandfather to distinguish wave patterns by how they felt against the hull. "If you can read the ocean, you will never be lost," Piailug taught his student.

Just as I began to wonder what Fred George does if it's snowing, the Web site narrative explains: "The elders do not travel in stormy weather." Of course not, I realized, recalling how often I'd regretted driving on snowbound roads in the mistaken notion that risking my life by going to work mattered more than staying home. A person who lives with nature rather than resists it doesn't ignore common sense; survival is a calculation constantly computing itself in the foreground.

If caught in a storm, Yup'ik travelers stop, construct a snow cave, and shelter within this artificial womb until the weather changes. "Skilled elders can predict the weather for the next 12 months," the narrative said, adding that this is why Yup'ik boys from the age of eight are told to study the weather at dawn and dusk. (For myself, I study the newspaper's five-day forecast despite a shocking lack of confidence in its accuracy.)

Different peoples learn what's most useful to their environment. Anthropologist Richard Nelson observed that Kutchin Athabascans living in the Arctic boreal forests found their way by memorizing geographical features, rather than referring to a night sky they couldn't see clearly. They didn't name very many stars or constellations; instead they oriented themselves around rivers or trails they'd established. They devoted themselves to learning the land around their individual traplines. "A man learns to find his way around in an area after a couple of years," Nelson writes, "but it takes much longer to become highly efficient as a hunter-trapper."

It's not that Native Alaskans are mysteriously endowed with abilities nobody else can cultivate. Not many of us learn such skills because our lives demand so few of them. (Without looking, do you know which phase the moon occupies at this moment?) Once technology seemed like magic, but when it fails us, how thrilling it is, how supernatural it seems when wayfinders conjure up the answers. In 2001, Anchorage searchers could not find a helicopter that had plunged into the opaque waters of Cook Inlet, which is complicated by tumultuous tides, strong winds, and strange currents. Two passengers were rescued, and the pilot's body was recovered the next day, but the bodies of two other people remained with the missing aircraft. After scientific instruments failed to locate the helicopter, an anthropologist suggested that searchers seek help from Dena'ina Athabascan elders who had fished these waters for decades. Leo Stephan, George Ondola, and Susie Ondola drew on their experiences and knowledge to successfully predict where the helicopter could be found.

But for all the mind's ability to reconcile a multitude of factors, surely every wayfinder must have experienced something like Nainoa Thompson did on his first voyage between Hawaii and Tahiti. Entering the doldrums in the double-hulled canoe meant sailing blind, because at that latitude, the nighttime clouds cloak the ocean in darkness so thick he couldn't see even the bow. Anxious and exhausted, he finally gave up and leaned against the ship's rail. "I felt this warmth come over me, and all of a sudden I knew where the moon was," he said. He gave directions for the canoe's movement to his crew with a confidence confirmed when the moon appeared briefly through a break in the clouds. That state of being is not something he can induce, he writes; it exists in a special realm beyond rational analysis.

There are questions I would ask Fred George. Has he ever been lost? Does it comfort him to know that if he were, the finest minds in his village could find him by reading every bit of information delivered by the sky, the land, the weather? What is it like to know that traveling alone under a December night sky is not an occasion for fear? How does it feel to be your own instrument of navigation, to travel with the eternal patience of Tunturyuk, to trust yourself?

Capt. Edward Glenn never explained why he himself did not lead the military detachment from the mouth of the Susitna River five hundred miles north to the Yukon River. But then, as commander of the U.S. Army's Cook Inlet Exploring Expedition of 1899, he wasn't obligated to do so. Instead, he used his official report to scorn the efforts of the men he sent. He noted icily that the expedition trekked as far as the Tanana Valley and then "lost heart because its members saw a comparatively insignificant swamp in front of them. The sight of this unexplored swamp, like the cry of 'mouse' to the average female, caused an ignominious and inexplicable flight."

A glance at the map, he said, told him that the detachment was closer to its goal of the Yukon River than to the army's station. If only the men had climbed to higher ground, or better yet, corduroyed a road with delimbed tree trunks, they certainly could have crossed any swamp. He hadn't bothered explaining such an obvious strategy beforehand, because "it was known that macadamized roads, paved streets, and railroad grades are not usually found in an unexplored country."

It is easy—and perhaps unfair—to imagine what his men must have thought of Glenn, comfortably established with his bed and food at Knik Station while they struggled through Alaska's worst traveling season, when the combination of soggy muskeg and tormenting mosquitoes creates a special kind of hell. No wonder Glenn was so irritated, though. His official report acknowledged that three of four detachments failed that year's mission to identify useful routes to the Interior's gold-fields. First, there was weakhearted Lt. George Van Schoonhoven and his men. Then, Sgt. William Yanert and Sgt. Frederick Mathys, sent to locate a trail along the Susitna River to Cook

Inlet, defied their orders and inexplicably left the lowlands to roam through the Talkeetna Mountains and down the glacial Matanuska River. The civilian topographer C. E. Griffith idiotically chose routes already traveled by army explorers.

Only Lt. Joseph Herron ascended through the Alaska Range and reached the Yukon. But first, he and his band of five were abandoned by their Native guides, became lost in the black spruce lowlands, had to cut loose their pack train, were compelled to build rafts, and then were forced to save themselves after the river destroyed the rafts. Wearing tatters and slowly starving as they wandered through the swamps, they were robbed of their remaining supplies by a bear, but it was the bear that saved them—rather, they were saved by the Athabascan chief, Sesui, who killed the bear. Upon discovering bacon in its belly, he recognized that white men must be about, backtracked the bear to find the exhausted explorers, and brought them to Telida, where they would recover for two months. Well fed, warmed by winter clothes, outfitted in snowshoes, assisted by dogs, and led by Indians, finally Herron and his men reached Fort Gibbons on the frozen Yukon just ten days before winter solstice.

If you unfold the detailed map that Herron produced after his harrowing journey, the stuttering lines and aureoles of hilltops don't reveal anything about what Herron really saw and felt and knew. "The map is not the territory," said anthropologist and social scientist Gregory Bateson, which any fool knows is true. But how I long to see Herron's life mapped on the page: the swamps of despair, the place where death almost caught up, the trail of generosity and hope.

In the old days the hypothetical geographers owned the world they themselves created on maps. It was these maps that sent explorers bumping along the west coast of North America in search of the Strait of Anian, the golden cities of Cibola, the great island of California. The fictional Northwest Passage preoccupied nations across four centuries. It was George Vancouver's particular pleasure to triumph over hypothetical geographers through his minute survey of Alaska's coasts, proving that if such a passage existed, it lay in polar realms. No matter: the internal maps of desire sent Arctic explorers to their frozen fates for another century until finally that most practical of explorers, Roald Amundsen, completed the Arctic passage between the Atlantic and Pacific oceans in 1905 and let everyone get some rest.

Alaska's military topographers and explorers knew the perils of maps made from lies. Lt. Joseph Castner remarked about the erroneous maps that misled him on his wretched journey from the coast to Interior Alaska, "It was only another instance of Alaskan mapmakers indulging their fancies in portraying the terrain of this region to the confounding and confusion of those who use the maps." He titled his official report "A Story of Hardship and Suffering in Alaska." In a speech he made, he quoted a similar complaint from Lt. Frederick Schwatka:

> *All Alaska is filled up in this way with rivers and their branches, even on government maps, that have yet to be traversed by white men in any capacity, let alone topography and survey. Probably the*

parlor authors of these maps think they are doing no more harm
than giving way to a too-eager desire of making out a full map.

These days, to resist the false hopes and expose the hidden purposes of modern maps, people engage in "groundtruthing." Companies equip vehicles with Global Positioning Systems so drivers can double-check reality, using their own eyeballs to confirm every stoplight, alley, intersection, and exit. Environmentalists walk through forests and study landscapes to reconcile what federal agencies want from timber sales with what actually exists.

It's possible to ground truth in history, too. A Tlingit man named Herb Hope did this after realizing that official accounts of the 1804 battle of Sitka between the Kiks.adi people and the occupying Russians did not reflect the version he heard from his uncles. He determined to look for the probable route taken by the Sheet'ka Kiks.adi on their Survival March from the battlefield. For several years, he and others tested various possibilities along beaches and through mountain passes on Baranof Island, until finally he successfully made a passage that helped him complete a story of resistance, honor, and endurance—one impossible to find on any map.

Even the excruciating detail of some maps won't help if you refuse to believe what you know to be true. I think of the hours I've spent studying topos, trying to imagine the actual degree of effort represented. Should we detour around that bog? That knot of elevation lines—surely that cliff isn't that steep? This stream will be a cinch to cross; probably you won't even have to take off your boots.

And time and time again, I have raised my eyes from the map's calm deceptions and realized how badly I have misjudged, how that blue filament means this uncrossable river, this gentle ridge is actually an evil sponge of high muskeg, the old trail promised by some dotted line has thieved itself away, if ever it existed. Figments and fictions, all of it. A friend and I once saved ourselves days of misery simply by checking our hiking route in the Brooks Range with someone who had traversed the valley we planned to cross. It's not that going that way would kill you, our groundtruther reported; you'll just want to kill yourselves halfway through that eternal plain of maddening tussocks. Even then, our better route came to naught on the very first day when winter arrived in early August. That blizzard was so mean it bent tent poles and sent us scurrying for the southern side of the range. No map ever cops to the ultimate verities of weather.

The greatest mystery is the way I'll continue lying to myself, over and over, a hypothetical geographer to the end, whose punishment and reward remains the need to bear witness myself, one blister, one dunking, one weary detour at a time.

I don't know any mapmakers except Sam Bishop. When he was a boy, his family lived for a few years at Lake Minchumina, to the west of Denali. His father, a wildlife biologist, photographed the mountain's white prominence from their cabin nearly every day for a year, and Sam and his brothers trapped, and ran dogs, and experienced a life that very few white people have known for a century or more. Like William Yanert, Sam was once compelled to map his home there. Though I cannot describe this marvelous portrait from memory, what persists is the notion that the legend might well have said, "This place I have come to know."

These days Alaska's web of land ownership is such sticky terrain that legions of maps exist to tell us what we can and cannot do, and where we can and cannot do them. Once Sam wrote to me about the government's attempts to define land by the way rural people live, based on whether their activities are "recreational" or "utilitarian." He wrote:

> When we lived at Minchumina, we often just explored. And we found useful things in the process—bear dens, moose ponds, old trails, berry patches, grouse gatherings, cabin log trees, lynx holed up for the winter in the upper end of a valley and thus easy to trap. We also found places of pure aesthetic interest (so far at least)—hidden knolls with fantastic views of Denali, a remnant grove of ancient white spruce that somehow escaped interior fires, a pond grown over with flowering buckbean, a vast new sandbar inviting a barefoot game of chase.
>
> How can you divorce the desire to find utility from the desire to find beauty?

Scores of maps of Alaska do that very thing, of course. That's what the army sought with its Herrons and Castners, its Allens and Abercrombies. They were sent to locate safer routes to the goldfields, to judge where familiar foods might grow, to identify the rivers and passes navigable for steamboats and trains, to find the places that would support settlers and those that would kill them. They were gathering "commercial intelligence," as one scholar puts it.

Once the army solved the major problems of geography, the efficient surveyors and topographers of the USGS worked in finer, utilitarian detail. Starting with the mining districts, they walked and measured and probed, and their maps are works of art modestly tucked into the cardboard pockets of their bulletins. They unfold like butterflies, colored in Cretaceous green, Jurassic blue, Paleozoic pink, Permian gray. These early maps are the philosophical extension of a purposeful government that figured out how to grid a landscape—hell, a continent—so that property and its resources could be parceled among the people who came, not the people who lived there. But the men who made them were the last true non-Native explorers of the North American continent, tough and diligent men who walked their way into their knowledge.

Since reading Sam's words, I have longed for the maps that a Herron or a Mathys might have drawn, honest in its joys and terrors, the maps not of discovery, but of knowingness. If only Van Schoonhoven had named that boggy valley "The Swamp Where Common Sense Prevailed" or maybe "The Place Where Captain Glenn Can Kiss My Ass." If only Yanert and Mathys had swaggered down the cobbled banks of the Matanuska River with sprigs of wild primrose tucked in their buttonholes, waving a seditious map of pleasure and pragmatism.

> *In this place we laughed to see infant bears tumbling through the snow.*
> *From this peak you will witness a sunset that is not to be believed.*
> *Along that bend the river achieves a lulling quality so as to make*
> *dreams easy.*
> *This pond is small but its waters so clear you can see the past and*
> *the future finning their way along the bottom.*

Strike north for the valley beyond survey lines and compass bearings,
where you can discover for yourself all these things and more besides.

Philosopher Mikhail Bakhtin invented the concept of the chronotope, which he described as "points in the geography of a community where time and space fuse. Time takes on flesh and becomes visible for human contemplation; likewise, space becomes charged and responsive to the movements of time and history and the enduring character of a people . . ." Anthropologist Thomas Thornton suggests that Tlingit names function as chronotopes; after all, Bakhtin noted that "language, as a treasure-house of images, is fundamentally chronotopic." I wonder, too, if the fascination some of us indulge with maps isn't a yearning to commemorate in our own lives those chronotopes, where "knots of narrative are tied and untied." The only true way to feel those moments is through groundtruthing, but the only way to convey their existence to others is to embed them in a story, even a story as thin as a map, as a technique of wayfinding.

In his book *Terra Cognita: The Mental Discovery of America*, Eviatar Zeruba argues that contact between Europeans and North America was a three-hundred-year process of mental discovery that ended only when Vitus Bering proved that Asia and North America were separate. Surely that process continues even now if people like Hope attempt again and again to locate those chronotopes where the bloody past and the restless present cannot be unknotted.

Once while visiting the USGS in Anchorage, I was horrified to see their stock of old maps for sale at a dollar each; people were buying them to use as wrapping paper. I bought one or two of each, feeling as if I were rescuing actual bits of terrain around Nome and Delta and Goodnews Bay and Jualin Mountain. Some charts revealed themselves as provisional, scrawled with surveyors' notes, as if the mapmakers' imaginations had not quite gelled the terrain into reality.

But these days, faced with a landscape that is changing more quickly than we can absorb, where this very moment permafrost melts, glaciers disappear, and ponds evaporate; where the coastline erodes and trees speed their northward march; where vanishing sea ice is drowning polar bears and freeing (at last!) the Northwest Passage; where the elders say time itself is accelerating, what are we to do with all these maps except remember a world that no longer exists? Every map lies. It lies. It lies.

Let us remember: it is the world itself that is provisional.

I can't draw maps, and I can barely follow them. But surely fragments of experience and words and images will some day assemble themselves like the leaves of an atlas, each page diagrammed and colored and infused with utility and beauty, so the way back will always remain clear. As an instrument of wayfinding, I am as dim-witted as the zipper-pull compass that companions and I once used to grope our way out of a rain forest when we realized we had no idea where we were. But if I substitute this chart of chronotopes for maps, how intensely, how precisely I am located:

An earthquake at dawn thrums the bones in my flesh as I lay belly down on a cold and barren shore of Glacier Bay.

A black bear stands beside me as I look toward the red cliffs above the Chulitna River, and the moment of silence before I recognize its presence vibrates between us even now.

Ravens kite overhead across that eternal threshold between day and night, light and dark.

High above the Copper River, my friends and I bathe ourselves at midnight in a cool pond, feet sinking into the mud, calves tickled by lily pads.

The jawbone of a moose presses into silt, the tracks of a pigeon-toed bear and her cub show their purposeful wander through dwarf fireweed, the hooves of caribou click as they step closer and closer, just to satisfy their curiosity.

Under a map-blue sky, I weep, and then I stand and hoist my pack and walk farther.

Because what else am I to do with all this discovering?

One year I climbed the blunt mountain behind our house every day for a month. That summer there would be no opportunity for a long excursion and no ready companion to join me, so a serial expedition seemed like an agreeable enterprise. The mountain measures 3,160 feet high, but the elevation gain is only 1,700 feet from the trailhead above Peters Creek. The path began in open aspen forest, wound through meadows, and switchbacked into a broad gully until ascending a slope so steep that sometimes it was easier to crawl on all fours than to stand. At the end I would heave myself over the ridge, eye-to-eye with a magenta patch of alpine azalea. The wind chilled my sweaty face, and the view of endless mountains behind me and the river plains beyond calmed that wild critter banging against my ribs. When it was time to leave, I would take great sliding steps downslope, sidehilling through blueberry bushes and skidding through moss, imagining how I would limp home with the sprain I risked each time. The next day I would do it all again.

Snow patched the top when I began May 17, and every day thereafter spring climbed with me, green creeping upward like mercury in a thermometer. I climbed in solitude, I climbed with companions, I climbed in the morning, and I climbed at midnight. I wished I had a dog to climb with me, but my two old dogs lay in rough graves ringed with stones at the foot of the mountain. Some days I bolted up and back within two hours. Other days I lingered, lying in spongy tundra thinking about nothing much, occasionally nibbling last year's sour cranberries. Sometimes I ascended within the moist blindfold of a cloud, but often my vision arced with the curvature of the earth toward the white fastness of Denali and its attendant peaks and glaciers. Usually I sang to myself and the bears (for surely there was a reason locals knew this as Bear Mountain), bellowing over and over the chorus from a Stan Rogers folk song: "Ah, for just one time, I would take the Northwest Passage, to find the hand of Franklin reaching for the Beaufort Sea, tracing one warm line through a land so wide and savage, and make a Northwest Passage to the sea . . ." Sometimes I walked silently.

Birds and flowers and trees made themselves known to me, and with determination I studied field guides and repeated names to myself. Each day's journey was different, but soon the path up the mountain began to seem like a well-paged story I could recite by heart. Marsh violets, twisted aspen, broomrape, the corner where I nearly collided with a moose's rear end, cat-erpillar alley, cow parsnip, false hellebore half-eaten by what? Golden-crowned sparrow and its melancholy minor triad, oxytrope and arnica, a splendid vision of Mount Susitna, the ground squirrel colony where I lost my watch, my footprints from the day before, and the day before that.

Halfway through this journey, so-called friends told me, if you can climb it thirty days in a row, you know you can climb it thirty-one. I cursed at hearing this, because it was true, and so I climbed thirty-one days, one after the other. That's if you count the only day I returned before reaching the summit because it seemed certain a bear lurked in the chute where alder thickets choked off vision. I do count that day because my knees did. They still remember every step taken on that fifty-one-thousand-foot mountain.

Though I thought of it always as Bear Mountain, this is not a name that appears on the USGS maps. Some consider the plateau as merely the ridge that leads to the bold pyramid of Mount Eklutna. One day I looked up the mountain in a book titled *Shem Pete's Alaska: The Territory of the Upper Cook Inlet Dena'ina*. This ethnogeography is a compilation of Athabascan names, maps, songs, and stories about this region, produced through thirty years of collaboration between two researchers, James Kari and James Fall, and numerous Dena'ina Athabascan elders, principally a remarkable geographer and storyteller named Shem Pete.

The triangular prow of Bear Mountain is identified in one of the photographs as Mount Eklutna, and the accompanying entry names it as *Snutnadzeni*, which translates to "That Which Extends Away Steeply." I'll say, I thought, remembering the uneasy thrill of standing at the plateau's northern rim where paragliders sometimes launched themselves beyond the rocky precipice. At the bottom lay two ponds most people call Mirror Lake and Edmonds Lake. The moment I read that their original names are *Snutnadzeni T'ugh Daydliyi Ben*, or "Lakes Beneath That Which Extends Steeply Away," instantly I recalled how from the ridge you could see, through the green lens of water, moose tracks dimpling the muddy bottom. Once I spotted a moose bobbing through the water like a miniature pool toy.

For hours I looked up every geographical feature I could think of, every one of them made new to me through their Dena'ina names. The book is not some obligatory nod to nostalgia with funny stories by old people; or a dusty artifact of distant, simpler times; or an academic exercise in linguistics. It is an atlas of how brilliantly the human mind can assemble knowledge of the world in a meaningful way, of how genius loci can reside within this life. The book's hardest lesson was in realizing how impossible it would be to absorb such knowingness across this vast distance of time and language, even from an atlas as wondrous as this.

In 1890, a professional adventurer named Edward James Glave and a packer named Jack Dalton canoed with the help of Yukon Athabascans down one of North America's great rivers. In accounts written for the expedition's sponsor, *Frank Leslie's Illustrated Newspaper*, Glave mistakenly identified this waterway as the Alsek, though most of his adventure took place on the Tatshenshini. I once rafted with a professional outfit on the Tat, so the Glave party's success in surviving this massive river in a cottonwood dugout is worth admiring. Raft guides say the river's challenge isn't in its few rapids or exciting wave forms but in its relentless power and volume. It's big water, with a potent will that gathers across 250 miles as it crosses the rolling terrain of the Yukon, plunges through the coastal massif, joins forces with the nearly unrunnable Alsek, passes broad blue glaciers, and then mildly braids itself across a delta and empties into the Pacific Ocean.

Glave neatly defined an explorer's mission as a "keen fascination in traveling through unknown lands; to be the first white men to erase from the map the hypothetical and fill up the blank area with the mountains, lakes, and rivers which belong to it." It was an impulse familiar to Robert Marshall, who, in the 1930s lovingly mapped the northern Koyukuk region of the Brooks Range with 137 previously unpublished names. He inhabited fully the explorer's essential paradox: intoxicated by blank maps, he promptly began de-blanking them by assigning names right and left, many of them his own invention.

But Glave cleverly sidestepped this paradox with a perspective unusual for his time. He told readers he'd use Native placenames whenever he could learn them. "In my opinion this should always be studied," he explained. "The Indian names of mountains, lakes, and rivers are natural landmarks for the traveler, whoever he may be; to destroy these by substituting words of a foreign tongue is to destroy the natural guides." Original names also should be preserved because "some tradition of tribal importance is always connected with them. These people have no written language, but the retention of their native names is an excellent medium through which to learn their history."

We all name things according to personal experience and local history. River guides on the Tat have created their own nomenclature, and during our ten-day trip we passed Cat in the Washing Machine Rapids and Purple Haze meadow and Monkey Wrench Rapids and the Center of the Universe, where the Tat and the Alsek combine forces in a great bowl of mountains. (A name of purely private meaning attaches itself to my memory: The Place Where That Running Moose Nearly Trampled Me in My Tent.)

But after reading the stories and descriptions by Shem Pete and his fellow experts, I finally understood the gulf between labeling maps and knowing place. Dena'ina names are not honorifics or memorials or historical placeholders. They refer to an intimate *shared* knowledge of the landscape and its providences and perils. Simply through their use, the names enlarge an understanding of the world, so that a person can locate himself not just geographically, but also culturally, historically, even cosmologically.

Yet in the Dena'ina dialect of the Upper Cook Inlet area (as with most other Athabascan dialects), the names present a pleasing solidity, even in translation: "Blocked by Rock" or "Creek Where There Is Mineral Pigment" or "Lake Where Game Trail Goes into the Water." But they also represent far more than a simplistic string of identifiers. The Athabascan system of grammatical construction extends layers of meaning that a nonspeaker like me can understand only secondhand. For example, as Kari and Fall explain, names can be assembled in clusters that help organize features geographically and explain their relationship. Important connections exist, for example, between *Dghelay Ka'a* or "Big Mountain" (Denali) and

Dghelishla, "Little Mountain" (Mount Susitna), as well as the ridges and hills that form ligaments among them. "A semantically linked set of names like this provides concrete and easily memorized images of the landscape from wherever it is viewed or discussed," write Kari and Fall. "Also it raises the question: is it possible that these names were planned out this way when they were first coined in the ancient past?"

Some names establish boundaries. Some embed traces of ancient movements through territories, and some share ideas with adjacent peoples, such as the Ahtna Athabascans of the Copper River Valley. A few names are pleasantly mystifying: "Where an Animal Is Crouching and Revolving" refers to how the Peters Hills near Denali look as a person circles them. Most names refer to animals, vegetation, terrain, geology, rivers, and aspects of natural history. A few recall customary activities or trails or important events, such as "River Where People Killed Each Other in Water" or "Where We Spend the Spring." But in examining almost six hundred names, the ethnographers found just six that refer to people, and only two of these to individuals.

In contrast, the roster of official geographic names, Donald J. Orth's *Dictionary of Alaska Place Names*, is stuffed with tributes to explorers' patrons, relatives, expedition members, European royalty, prospectors. Though Cook Inlet and Prince of Wales Island and Miller Creek and Bucareli Bay and Shishmaref Island and Philip Smith Mountains say interesting things about recent history, they are not intimate or useful; they mean almost nothing to anyone walking this earth today. Mount McKinley, known to the Koyukon Athabascans as *Deenaalee* ("The High One"), was named by a prospector in 1896 for an obscure Ohio senator who championed the gold standard, but just try convincing the current senators from Ohio to allow Alaska to change the name to the anglicized version, Denali. Legions of common references to gold, geographical features, and animals abound; there are at least eleven Bear Mountains, and scores of Sheep Thises and Goat Thats. Some explorers, like Herron, did their best to record Native names, though few survive in recognizable form. Oddly, the most prominent Anchorage feature identified with a Dena'ina story is Mount Susitna, or Sleeping Lady, but the band of elders consulted by Kari and Fall said they had never heard the romantic legend most everyone attaches to this mountain's supine shape.

The Athabascan approach to names and places is similar to practices of other original peoples, of course. When non-Native researchers from federal agencies embarked on a project to locate historical and cemetery sites in southwestern Alaska, they wrestled with many cultural and philosophical difficulties, not the least of which was the Yup'ik response that "the whole river is a historical site!" as researcher Robert Drozda reported hearing many times. The complexity of understanding, remembering, and relating such information from one generation through the next was demonstrated by elders such as Joshua Phillip, who mapped from memory the important places and burial sites in a river drainage of approximately four hundred square miles. "USGS maps of the same area record seven names; six are incorrect," Drozda commented. "Mr. Phillip recorded thirty-three place names and numerous hydrological features not shown on official maps. During a more in-depth survey in 1988 elders recorded over one hundred place names in the same area." More importantly, they could describe the meaning of such names, filling those brightly lit rooms where the researchers and elders worked with the presences of many generations before them.

In Southeast Alaska, anthropologist Tom Thornton worked with an eighty-three-year-old Tlingit elder named Herman Kitka, Sr., to document more than two hundred place-names. In keeping with the Tlingit custom, the pattern of names extends across one thousand miles "as Raven flies," and radiates along two important axes: how people structured themselves socially and how they organized their efforts around the cycle of food gathering. At every major level of Tlingit identity, people link themselves specifically to a place, whether they speak of themselves as a nation, as a member of one of two major matrilineal groups of clans (the Raven and the Wolf/Eagle moieties), or as a member of those groups dwelling in a particular region, known as a kwaan. Even local clan identity usually refers to a group's origin and distribution, Thornton writes, so that people who have migrated some distance in time and place renew their connection every time they name their clan or their house group. When Kitka identifies his moiety, kwaan, clan, and house, he's also referring to a history of how his people came to be where they live and what property rights they claim to local fish, berries, shellfish, game, marine mammals, and even stories, songs, and crests. "What is more, the linguistic construction of such clan names evokes a sense of belonging or being possessed by the named place," Thornton notes. ". . . Thus, we cannot speak of the Kiks.adi without implicitly invoking their ties to Helm Bay (Kiks), the place for which they are named." To name a place, then, is also to invoke its link to the people and to a history extending into Raven's time.

Imagine gathering forty-five residents from a region similar in size to the territory where Dena'ina dialects were once spoken. Ohio or Tennessee will do. Now ask these good people to identify the location and history of a thousand places known to them in common—not easy stuff like freeways and cities, but creeks and hills and lakes and river bends and bluffs and ridges, all the places that feed them and clothe them and save them. How quickly their voices—our voices—would falter.

Dena'ina lexicography represents a way to organize not just words, not just place, but life itself. "Consider that the last speakers of the Upper Cook Inlet dialect of Dena'ina who have reported names for this book learned about them while traveling in the country or, in some cases, from listening to stories," Kari writes. "The speakers report these place names with great care and with obvious affection from the associations between the names, the ancestors, and the land." Shem Pete knew more than 650 of the 973 place-names listed and had traveled to most of those places by boat or by foot, journeying through an area of almost fourteen thousand square miles.

Dena'ina do not add new names to this memory bank; if a name has died, it lies fallow. The original names were meant to persist, to express patterns, to travel accurately through the only conduit that can cross time, which is the human mind. Though early Native geographers could accurately draw on paper their knowledge when asked to do so, it was the act of naming that allowed names to survive beyond the static media of maps and books. About sixty Dena'ina names were recorded before 1845, Kari reports, and 150 years later Shem Pete and his contemporaries knew all but five or six of them.

The problem is, of course, that the chain of human minds is so easily ruptured. Among events Shem Pete recalled were three waves of plague that swept through villages on the lower Susitna River: whooping cough, measles, and the flu of 1918 that killed six hundred people, including his mother. "Gee whiz, we get pretty lonesome," he said in reciting this litany of decimation. "We're only a few people left." Shem Pete, born around 1896, honored and respected by Dena'ina and non-Natives, died in 1989, followed by his son, Billy, in 1995. "In 2003 we can report that there is only a small number of older generation speakers in the Upper Inlet, Outer Inlet, and Iliamna dialects," Kari and Fall write. "The Inland dialect has fewer than fifty speakers."

The erosion of names throughout Alaska represents these greater losses. Any map of Cook Inlet blithely reveals the dimensions of this familiar story. Prospectors, trappers, and settlers arrived, built roads and towns, fished and hunted on Dena'ina lands, yet never knew the original names of the prominent bands or even their names in translation: the Peninsula People, the Beach People, the People Who Holler to Make Migrating Birds Fall Down, the Mountain People and Small Timber People, the Headwaters People and Good Land People, and all of the other people.

The land itself erodes, in identity, in purpose. In the 1990s, Eklutna villagers successfully protested when the Bank of Alaska received a permit to quarry rock from mounds already mined for decades by the Alaska Railroad. The Dena'ina called these hillocks The Knobs, but the name contemporary Athabascans used referring to both in relationship to the Eklutna River was *Idluytnu*, "Two Things Laying by the River." In the old days these navigational landmarks meant you were almost home, and they served as lookouts for game and for enemies. What non-Natives saw as a source of gravel, Eklutna elders regarded as just as important to their identity as any monument in Washington, D.C. Lee Stephan explained it this way: "How important to a person's face is his nose?"

Now and then I saw other people hiking up Bear Mountain, but we always passed each other with a nod or quick greeting, never had much of anything to tell each other.

The phrase used for the kind of life the Dena'ina knew is "living off the land," but in reading the names of these places, the struggle for survival reveals its sharp teeth. When Shem Pete finished recording a story, Fall says, he would mention how important the story was, "and that people should know that story because some day they might hear that story and they might save their lives with that story." How naturally that impulse transmitted itself, even to me, a middle-aged non-Native woman never truly hungry in her life. Yet now I know where to go should I need to make needlefish soup. I learned this reading Shem Pete's descriptions of *Dgheyay Leht*, "Stickleback Creek," which is known today as Ship Creek and is the site where Anchorage's original tent city was established in 1915. When people starved after a long winter, before the smelt and the king salmon started running, they would "drag" themselves to the creek and fill up on needlefish. "At that *Dgheyay Leht* we save ourselves nicely," he recalled. On an island near the mouth of the Susitna, there's *K'tl'ila T'el'iht,* "Where Indian Potato Is Gathered," and there's *Sheshnena,* "Saving Land," in that direction, too. "All you need is a little hook and some snares to survive in that country," said Shem Pete's son, Billy. "We caught lots of big grayling and spruce grouse."

Though no need to save myself has presented itself so far, somehow it matters to know that before the arrival of the military base and McDonald's, and the airport and the subdivisions, in all these places and more, people netted salmon and gathered eggs, hunted porcupine and caught geese, trapped beaver and pulled trout, that in the mountains where Anchorage residents hike for fun, the Dena'ina killed moose and sheep, that all of this was for life not sport, that if we understood the true names of these places we would know these things, too.

The mountain filled me even when I didn't push myself up its flanks, but eventually that inner presence subsided as my attention turned elsewhere. I haven't returned to climb Bear Mountain since I moved thirty miles away into the Anchorage Bowl, where many other mountains deserve climbing, too.

And now I wonder: Why didn't I spend even a night there alone? Why did I measure my effort in elevation, and not in hours, days, months, lifetimes? Why couldn't I build a little hut, live there for the remaining eleven months of spring, of summer, of fall, of winter, all those mountain months about which I know nothing at all?

Yet even another eleven months would never be enough, because beyond them lies season after season, year after year, a lifetime of reaching for an understanding that would extend steeply before me, forever beyond my reach. And even if I learned to pronounce properly the mountain's true name, *Snutnadzeni, Snutnadzeni, Snutnadzeni,* and understand without labored thought its delicate layers of meaning, to whom would I say such a name so that it mattered?

One afternoon while shuffling through the strata of papers and stones and books in my office, my eye fell upon a folded paper square. Pierced instantly by yearning, I recognized in its whorls and creases a crude map of the Fairbanks-Circle Trail. Or is it the Circle-Fairbanks Trail?

Next time, I thought, I should begin at the other end. Perhaps a friend would go; maybe I could persuade my husband to join me. The other day he said that I'm an "around-the-bender," compelled to go just a little farther, and then a little farther still, if only to see what lies beyond. I didn't tell him this, but I've been lucky enough in life to sleep at three Centers of the Universe: at the confluence of the Tatshenshini and Alsek rivers; in the vast basin where Miles and Childs glaciers flank the Copper River; and in our bed at home, where he is always waiting for me to return.

Reading a friend's book, it occurred to me how peopled her travels are, and how lately my own small journeys turn toward solitude, as if it were the missing point on the compass rose. The one Athabascan word that sticks in my head is *gheyul*: to seek by walking. "You wouldn't go alone if you had children," a man said to me once. For a fact, I am so alone that I will never know if that's true. What I don't say aloud is my suspicion that all this is merely a way to practice for the journey that everyone makes alone, the one story whose ending nobody ever knows.

But my blue heeler, Bix, is a year old now, a fearless stream-crosser who has already rousted a brown bear and run away as fast as his puppy legs would take him from that fortunately amiable creature. He's sensible that way. He has his own pack; he could wear Jenny's bell. He's more rambunctious and stubborn than she was—a black pirate's patch marking his right eye says everything you need to know about his personality—but he loves me just as fiercely as she did. Over the long winter there will be time to test the instruments of navigation, study the maps, sort gear, plan meals, decide whether to fix up this aching knee first, imagine how the trip might go wrong and how good it will feel to finish that trail at last, if not next year, then some year not too far away. This imagining, this longing, is a kind of wayfinding, too.

Rummaging through past experiences on that old route, I remembered the false paths and the doubts that beset me and the painful decision to turn around. This time, I thought, my dog and I will take all the time we need, and we will get there when we get there, and we will come home tired and happy. We'll leave the maps behind, because they don't say much except where you started and where you'll end if you're lucky. The rest of it, I suppose, we'll discover as we walk, naming our way across the land.

Acknowledgments

I'VE BEEN LUCKY TO HAVE the finest of companions on these and other journeys in Alaska and in life. They inspired me through difficulties, discouragement, and fears real and imagined, and they've each taught me something about how to be a better person and a true adventurer. They include Sam Bishop, Richard Steele, Hank Lentfer, Frank Soos, Mark Kelley, and Jennifer Brice. If they are not fully named in these stories, it's only because their stories belong to them, not to me. Thanks also to Sam and Hank for thoughtful comments. Some of the most fun I've ever known has been in the adventuresome company of Thea "Cheese Monkey" Agnew, Lynn Hallquist, Butch "Bacon" Allen, Lila Vogt, Kari Barnard, Nancy Cook, David Grimes, Nora Gruner, Martha Bristow, Kris Capps,

Debbie Carter, and Tricia Brown. Here's to more camping trips, river floats, and glacier crossings in our futures. Sara Rufner, Dawnell Smith, Liz Bradfield, and Martha Bristow climbed Bear Mountain with me and kept me company. Some of these treks could not have been made without the help and sometimes the forbearance of Kris Capps, Craig Jones, Al Brice, Joe Durrenberger, and Charles Mason. Thank you.

Joanne Wyckoff helped reinvigorate this manuscript through insightful suggestions. Elizabeth Wales provided early encouragement, and Terrell Dixon has been a wonderful influence. Richard Carstensen and Kim Heacox offered good advice at important crossroads. I'm grateful to Gary Luke for wise advice, and to Kurt Stephan, Lauren Kennedy, and Karin Mullen for their keen editorial eyes.

The Common Counsel Foundation gave me the great gift of the Mesa Refuge, at which some of this book was finished.

Robert Meyerowitz, a generous and rigorous editor, helped make every piece that he published better. Lynne Snifka saved me from myself more than once. They're good friends, besides. Thanks for various editorial ministrations and invitations to Amanda Coyne, Kyle Hopkins, Susan Fox Rogers, Bill Sherwonit, Andromeda Romano-Lax, Ellen Bielawski, Carolyn Kremers, Anne Hanley, and especially Kathy Tarr.

Peggy Shumaker and Joe Usibelli are an inspiration, in art and in friendship. Anne Caston is the best of colleagues and a model of dedication to writing and teaching. Carol Swartz, Rich Chiappone, Eva Saulitis, and Nancy Lord have made Homer feel like a second home, through their words and their friendship.

Trudy Christopher is the most entertaining and supportive of correspondents, not to mention an endless source of arcane information, and I'm grateful to her for reminding me not to give up, particularly when crossing a muskeg seemed more appealing than rewriting a paragraph one more time. "Every landscape has its solaces," she once remarked, and that's true of the landscape of the page as well. Ernestine Hayes has the gift of double vision and is always teaching me something important.

Family and friends endured more tales and photographs than anyone should. Thanks especially to Connie and Erik Hulbert for putting me up and putting up with me so many times for so many trips. Ken Simpson has been a wonderful reader. Jo-Ann Mapson, Stewart Allison, and the Insane Clown Posse have kept me from going insane myself many times. No one could ask for better or more talented friends.

I am greatly indebted to explorers and adventurers past and present, known and unknown, and to the writers who have thought so deeply about landscape and history. I am painfully aware that I do not do any of them justice. Their own words are the best testament to their accomplishments.

There is no better friend on the trail than a good dog. They never lose heart. I've had three: Jenny, Jick, and Bix.

Scott Kiefer has accompanied me on every step of the most perilous journeys I've known. He is the love of my life and the reason I know where home is.

About the Author

SHERRY SIMPSON teaches creative writing at the University of Alaska Anchorage and the Rainier Writing Workshop at Pacific Lutheran University. She grew up in Juneau and worked as a newspaper reporter in Fairbanks and Juneau before writing her first collection of essays, *The Way Winter Comes: Alaska Stories*. She and her husband live in Anchorage.